erotic literature
of ancient india

EROTIC LITERATURE OF ANCIENT INDIA

KAMA SUTRA . KOKA SHASTRA
GITA GOVINDAM . ANANGA RANGA

Sandhya Mulchandani

Lustre Press
Roli Books

contents

❦

dedication

To the wise men of ancient India who considered
satisfaction in every sphere of life to be a characteristic
of civilized society. Unburdened by hypocrisy or
duplicity, they believed that sensual indulgence was a
sacred duty and that all human emotions should be
tastefully expressed and gracefully experienced.

INTRODUCTION:
Sublimo beatitudo

Civilization is at a stage of development where the quest for happiness can surely not be overlooked or underestimated. The perceived sense of happiness and contentment that material goods can bring, have sustained politics and economies and can even justifiably be the rationale behind why empires developed and kingdoms flourished. The satisfaction resulting from the acquisition of lands and armies, gold and goods or even women has been the cause of confrontations since time immemorial. The elusive and illusionary quest for happiness that acquisitions are supposed to ensure occupies so much of our ambitions and waking thoughts that they have been the subject of serious study from the earliest of times. Religion and science have striven to understand and gain control over all that is mysterious and incomprehensible.

According to ancient wisdom this quest for pleasure and happiness, albeit metaphysical rather than merely physical, was the springboard for all human action. The Greek philosopher Aristotle (384-322 BC) described happiness as the active fulfilment of natural capacities. Epicurus too believed that happiness was the highest ideal, and the

ultimate goal in life. Indians too viewed happiness as a prerequisite for existence, and the pursuit and understanding of pleasure and happiness known as *sukha* became a subject of rigorous inquiry.

According to the claims of most religions, creation has a meaning and purpose, and at its core equates God with love. We get glimpses of the sublime nature of beauty, truth and goodness at rare moments in, perhaps, art or nature or when we love or are loved by others. But just what is it about happiness that holds out such value? Why was the pursuit of happiness considered to be almost a revered duty? Ancient philosophers purported to have an answer: they believed that since no man deliberately chose to be unhappy it was an unnatural state of being and had been forced on mankind because of his separateness from the Primal Being—ever since he was symbolically thrown out of the Garden of Eden. The search for happiness and bliss was thus considered to be a return to one's natural state. According to the *Upanishads*, creation was suffused with *sukha* or joy as both a reflection and attribute of the Infinite. The *Chandogya Upanishad* says: 'Where there is joy, there is creation. Where there is no joy, there is no creation: know this to be the nature of joy.' And again in the *Taittiriya Upanishad*, the seeker of truth finally understands the mystery of Brahman: '…and then he saw that Brahman was joy: for from joy all beings have come, by joy they all live, and unto joy they all return.' The purpose of life, believed the ancients, was thus to transform all latent human energies and manifest them in a search for a higher consciousness, which in Hinduism came to be known as *Sat-Chit-Ananda* that loosely translates as Pure Existence, Pure Consciousness and Pure Bliss. The bedrock of Hindu philosophy is that one can realize and experience so much spiritual ecstasy that material pleasures fade into insignificance. Thus the source of all happiness, ecstasy, love and bliss—the penultimate quest of every human being—is God. These concepts were not confined only to Hinduism. Rather it was almost a universal phenomenon. The Greeks, for example, believed that there was a four-fold path to bliss and that happiness had four levels. The first level was called *laetus* or happiness that was got by extraneous factors. This was necessarily short-lived and left one wanting for more. The second was *felix* which meant happiness of comparative advantage. This kind of happiness was based on how we measured up to others, and was again rather unstable and could lead to unhappiness and sense of worthlessness. The third was called *beatitudo,* the happiness that comes from seeing the good in others and doing good for others. The final one was *sublimo beatitudo* which was perfect happiness and therefore, filled with goodness, beauty, truth and love—the ultimate happiness which is found in a relationship with God.

In a similar vein, long before the Greeks, Indian philosophy described the immediate goal of all sentient beings as seeking happiness, the final beatitude being known as *mahasukha* or *ananda,* better described as bliss. This word is also used to describe the *Parabrahman* or the Supreme Being. This blissful state, it was thought, could be achieved through both mystical and aesthetic experiences. From the earliest times, Indian philosophy has always believed that fulfilment and happiness in life are a result of the sacred fusion of the body, mind and soul. There are just as many paths to seek this *paramananda* or ultimate bliss as there are gods in India. Many of these paths, however, are esoteric and shrouded in mystery.

The basic belief as articulated in the *Taittiriya Upanishad* (700 BCE), is that there were seven worlds or planes of consciousness and existence. The lower three—the physical, vital, and mental—were planes of finite existence, while the higher four were transcendent planes that lead to Infinite Consciousness and Bliss. Beyond all these planes was of course 'the Supreme' or 'the Absolute.' Variously called *bhuloka* (the earthly plane), *mahaloka* (the greater plane), *Brahmaloka* (the world of Brahma), to name a few. In Hindu cosmology, these worlds referred to the manifold experiences that one goes through during a lifetime and were built up in an ascending order. Therefore various stages of finding *ananda* or bliss were named after the abode of the gods (who themselves have a hierarchy) and were variously called *Ratianand, Brahmanand, Indranand,* among others. It was believed that different desires found expression and fulfilment in various stages of experiences starting from worldly experiences as in the *bhuloka* right up to the happiness experienced in *Brahmaloka* which

❉ *Facing page:* The penultimate quest of every human being is God who personifies perfect happiness, beauty, truth and love. The pathways to God many differ from each other but the essential quest remains the same.

was said to be the bedrock of the highest plane of realization.

The sense of sacredness in the Other is the hallmark of Indian philosophy and permeates through every aspect of mental and physical existence. Being a religion both porous and permissive, Hinduism makes it possible to explore all human emotions and uses these very same sentiments as a means to seek a spiritual life. Foremost among these was sexuality, which the ancients in India saw as an intrinsic component of human life and

It was thus believed that an orgasm most closely simulated the absolute bliss that human beings consciously or unconsciously strived for, and this pleasure though ephemeral, created a momentary state of balance and oneness with a higher being. Underlying these sexual experiences is a spiritual angle, one that attempts to explain the true relationship between man and woman—the dual principle of *purusha-prakriti* in the metaphysical sense. The entire creation is seen as manifestation and eternal

almost a sacred duty. Since they believed that creation was simultaneously both sacred and sensual, the pleasures of the human body became yet another accepted path of contemplating spiritual union. Therefore sex, love and intimacy were approached as a religious and an artistic ritual, a means to strike the right balance between all urges: physical, emotional, intellectual, social, sexual as well as spiritual.

play, where man is *purusha* and woman, *prakriti*. *Purusha* is the *sakshi* or witnessing aspect of the Divine, enjoying the multiplicity of *prakriti*'s manifestations. This provides a debatable but quasi-metaphysical explanation for the innate tendency of women to lose their identities with unreserved self-giving. It is this search for the union of soul with soul, the fusion of divine with divine that results in *ananda* in which

✤ *Above:* The entire creation is seen as a manifestation and eternal play or *lila*, where man is the *purusha* and woman is *prakriti*.

lies the ultimate fulfilment of the union of man and woman.

From the times of the Vedas, the *Upanishads* to the epic Mahabharata that has at least 40 long chapters devoted to investigating the sexual impulse, sexuality has been a subject of study. This, coupled with the eternal quest for bliss paved the way to the detailed study of man's creative energies. The perspective on sexuality of an entire society was one of awe and wonder—that the ability of a man and a woman coming

together and creating another human being, seemingly out of nothing, was magical. The need to fully comprehend, explore and sustain these magical moments became an end in itself. Curiosity led to contemplation, and the study of human sexuality became a basis for human existence, the thread of sexuality woven deep into its fabric.

Hindu philosophy has often been rebuked for being otherworldly, with followers often depicted in cross-legged and cross-eyed trances. This stereotype sidesteps one seminal point: the vital engagement of its religion with the mundane world to such an extent that it does not eschew desire but includes it as one of the aims of life and fulfilment. The Hindus did not confine themselves to the study of love in isolation, but explored the entire range of refinements that made life worthwhile. According to ancient wisdom, the life of a human served a three-pronged goal (*trivarga*): the striving for good *dharma* or

right conduct, useful *artha* or material possessions and well-being, and *kama* or love and its associated pleasures of the senses.

Even ascetics of the highest order accepted that every aspect of human emotion had to be explored and experienced, for only then could one successfully transcend it. Sexuality was, along with *dharma* and *artha*, accepted as one of the four *purusharthas* (goals of life) whose knowledge was needed

Above: The ultimate fulfilment of the union between man and woman is the quest of the union of soul with soul, the fusion of divine with divine that results in *ananda*.

Following pages 14-15: Sexuality is an integral part of human existence, to be celebrated instead of repressed or denied altogether.

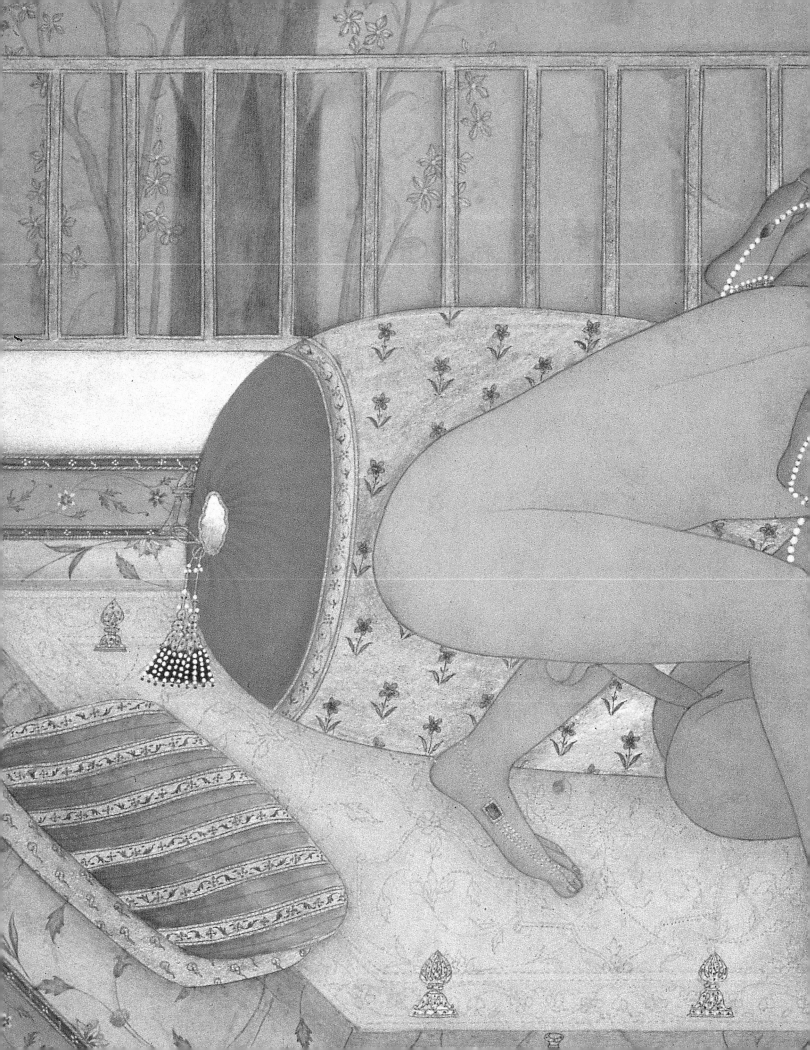

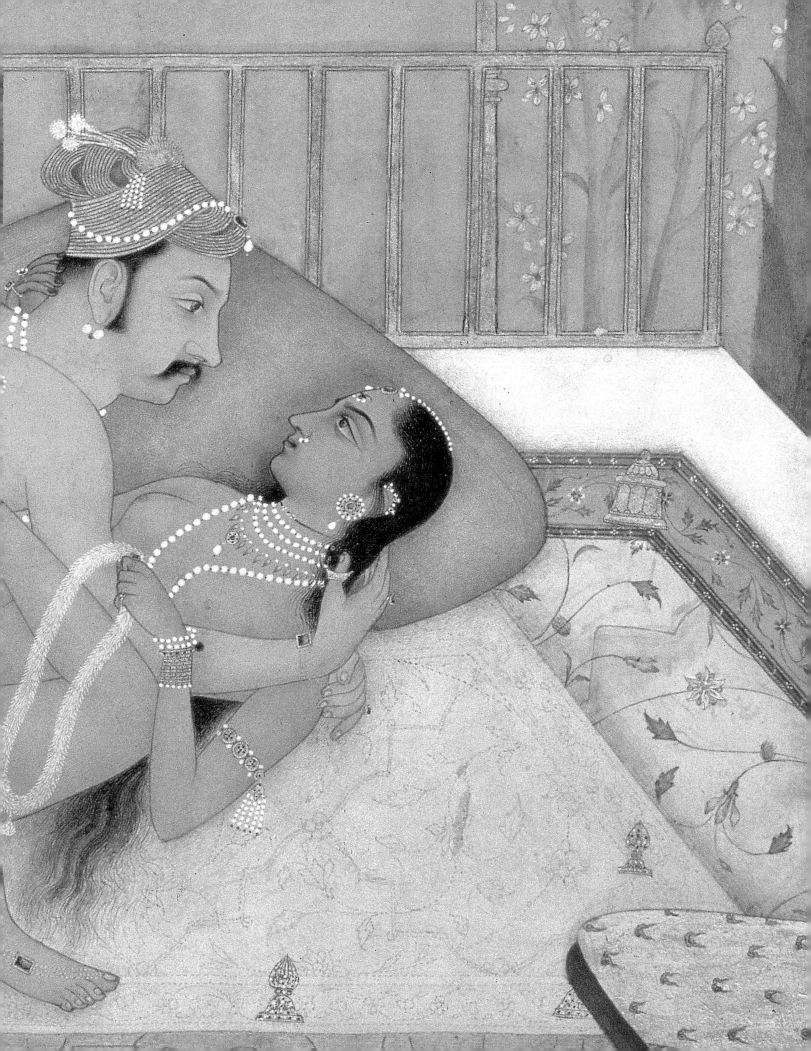

❋ 'O Radha! I gaze upon your beautiful face, which is like a blossoming lotus in the lake of pure love, a lotus decorated with the black bees of the curling locks of hair, a face that is a moon bringing tidal waves to the nectar ocean of bliss.'

16

❋ 'O Radha, treasure of bliss! When the best of lovers falls at your feet and begs for the sweet nectar of a single embrace, should I see you knit your eyebrows and hear you say "No! No!" '

if a balanced life was to be achieved. By weaving these aspects into the right combination, one could discover the meaning and beauty of life and relationships. The stress was on integration: neglecting one of these areas would lead to diminished stability and a dangerous imbalance in man. The senses were thus perceived as being a refinement of the physical on a higher plane of consciousness, sex forming an integral part of a full and complete life.

The most accepted path of seeking the divine was the path of spirituality and total devotion to the chosen god. This was known as the *bhakti yoga*—the yoga of devotion to God. The other was the path of acquired wisdom known as *gyana yoga*. The Hindu ideal of God, much like the western monotheistic religions is of One Being, of One God who is the unifying factor of all creation. But as each desire became personified, idolized as a god worthy of worship, numerous personal gods arose, thereby yielding separate entities. One such deity was Krishna. The manifestation of God as Krishna included a vast emotional range—love, devotion, friendship, statesmanship, to name just a few.

The other personal god in whom a range of human emotions became embodied was Shiva, considered to be the destroyer of evil and sorrow. As *Nataraja* he is the Divine Cosmic Dancer; as *Ardhanarishwara*, he is both man and woman. He is both static and dynamic, creator and destroyer as well as the source of fertility in all living beings. He is as fierce as he is gentle, merciful and compassionate.

Shiva is also inseparable from his feminine creative energies known as *Shakti;* while Shiva is conceptualized as masculine and pure consciousness, existence and bliss, *Shakti* is the female, dynamic, energetic, creative aspect of consciousness. There is no Shiva without *Shakti* and no *Shakti* without Shiva: the two are the absolute state of being, consciousness and bliss. The wedlock of Shiva and Parvati, a manifestation of *Shakti,* thus opened as it were the portals to the world's bliss.

The other god who evokes absolute devotion is Krishna, the eighth incarnation of Lord Vishnu who epitomizes knowledge and pure existence, consciousness and bliss. Myriad tales are told about Krishna who is acknowledged to be the *poornavatar* or the complete man. He is a mischievous child, a trouble-causing teenager, an amorous adolescent, a lover beyond compare, a friend, husband, advisor, as well as a formidable enemy. In India, Krishna continues to live on as an unquestioned presence in the daily lives of millions of people, participating in their hopes and joys, sorrows and grief, in song and dance, music and art, in festivals and ceremonials, in laughter and gaiety, effortlessly merging his often divergent aspects as lover and god. This *ananda* or joy that was realized by knowing Krishna became the leitmotif of what has come to be known as the *rasa lila* or Krishna's interplay with the *gopis* or cowherd girls. The *rasa lila* thus became an affirmation of the sexual as a window to the divine. The love story of the *gopis* and Krishna is celebrated in Indian classical music, in the devotional songs of medieval *bhaktas* and a long line of bards and

❋ *Facing page:* 'Radha, you are a goddess with curly black hair, glistening bimba-fruit like lips, a moonlike face, playful eyes like the Khanjana bird, broad hips, a slender waist, splendid breasts, and vine-arms decorated with graceful armlets.'

॥रागणि बिलावल। यब जीहरपति यी षदे तुषम्प हरति श्रृंग प्रमरतका
मधुबेनद्यु तालतमालविरंग।१९

✤ Temple sculpture featured *maithuna* or loving couples as well as erotic and copulating men and women as the emphasis was on exploring the tender nuances of the romantic emotion.

✽ The romantic emotion in the classical period was best expressed in the visual arts. Oral poetry found a spatial dimension in *shilpa* or sculpture that flourished in temples.

21

balladeers, most of whom drew inspiration from the 12th-century Sanskrit poet, Jayadeva: he decisively shaped the legend's outlines. The *Gita Govindam* describes in vivid detail the love affairs of Krishna with the *gopis* and his secret love for Radha.

The aim of erotic works in Indian literature such as the *Kama Sutra* was to deal comprehensively with the aspects of pleasure and love. According to certain hypotheses, *kama* teachings came into existence because of frustration in the married life of a couple in a patriarchal society where marriages were arranged for convenience and marriages of love were uncommon. *Kama* literature was written in a technical format and is thought to have been for people of the higher castes because the social structure of the time permitted very little private time for a husband and wife. Sexual relations were seen as the only permissible token of affection a husband could show his new bride; at the same time, sex was a source of anxiety because it was the only activity privately shared by the couple and stood as the grounds on which the relationship was based.

So the ancients studied sex, practised and dissected it, classified its many methods, shared their knowledge about techniques and passed on what they had learnt. Erotology became a science of not merely exploring the physicality of intercourse but examining its pleasures and pitfalls—*sringara,* the art of adornment, the sixty-four branches of fine arts, virility and aphrodisiacs, etiquette and manners, townsmen and courtesans—covering every conceivable aspect of society.

The best known of the *kama* literature is of course Vatsyayana's *Kama Sutra,* compiled around the third century CE. It is a technical account of the social structure, dealing with manners, morals, sexology, and culture in the third century. He states that much of the condemnation of sexual practices is due to abnormal expressions and perversions rather than due to a healthy concern for it. Vatsyayana also maintains that 'sexual satisfaction, like food, is essential to the maintenance of bodily health' and 'though evil effects may follow as a result of indulgence, passion has to be appeased.' Therefore, he urges the study of the *Kama Shastras* in order to achieve the fullness of pleasure that only humans can obtain in sexual union.

Besides literature, such a wide and varied spiritual platform lent itself to telling and brilliant images in art. The *Kama Sutra* inspired artists to explore every corner of the human psyche and all the platforms where social discourse on pleasure takes place—the kingly court, the noble's mansion, the maiden's boudoir, the secret garden, the moonlit night… . These stages were most poetically portrayed in Indian miniature painting, based on the theory of *rasa.* In its widest sense, *rasa* is the depiction of a mood that matches one of the nine essences of life—the *navarasas.* The *rasa* theory is the bedrock of Indian art and nowhere is it seen as vividly as in Indian miniature painting which became a potent medium for the expression of visual fantasies. The depiction of the *nayika* or a very beautiful young woman in her myriad moods as she goes out to meet her lover or *nayak,* the anticipation on the face of a lover who is waiting for his beloved, the sexual energies during intercourse, were all noted and expressed in minute detail. Nature

of unspoiled romance and eroticism. - Research into erotology flourished, and following in the footsteps of the *Kama Sutra,* latter-day texts were written in accordance with the social and moral norms of the times. Texts like *Rati Rahasya* also known as the *Koka Shastra,* the *Ananga Ranga,* the *Ratimanjari,* the *Ratiratnapradipika,* the *Panchasayaka,* the *Nagarasarvasvam,* to name just a few, spanning nearly a thousand years, focused on acquiring the right knowledge about the physicality of love that in turn

provided the backdrop against which much of this human drama was enacted. Birds and bowers, rain-filled clouds and vines and most importantly the coming of *phalgun* or spring that was seen as the playing ground of Kamadev, the God of Love himself, were all depicted with loving grace by Indian artists to convey a sense of joy and wonder, a mood

would lead to experiencing bliss. Besides erotic treatises, some of the best literature suffused as it were with the erotic sentiment came forth from India's most celebrated poet and dramatist, Kalidasa. An ardent devotee of Goddess Kali, as his name suggests, Kalidasa was rewarded with the gift of the pen and infinite wisdom, making him the most

✤ *Above:* 'All I know is that he came here
Smiling that smile of his
And took me by the hand
But I know nothing of those violent red lips
Pressed on mine.'

brilliant of the 'nine gems' at the court of Vikramaditya of Ujjain. Taking their cue from Kalidasa, numerous other writers and poets followed, successfully merging the sacred with the sensual raising both art and faith to new heights.

The deceptively simple *Gita Govindam* written in the latter part of the 12th century earned sainthood for its writer Jayadeva and a wide audience for his poem. The *Gita Govindam* reaches the acme of sublime love between a man and a woman. Replete with

lyrical religious eroticisms, its twelve cantos ushered in a new era in Indian literature. No one was above the influence and power of sexuality. India's foremost exponent of Hindu Advaita philosophy, Adi Shankaracharya, conceded that all aspects of human life had to be understood and explored before one could even hope to attain a state of *ananda*.

To this end he is credited to have penned an extremely erotic set of hundred poems called the *Amarusataka*.

The period between the 14th and 17th centuries saw one of the most refined and productive stages in the development of Indian literature. Ranging from devotional quatrains and *bhakti kavyas* to court poetry and erotic love songs, this period dealt with a wide range of poetics like devotion, religious fervour, *rasa, alankara* (adornment) and *sringara*. Writing without dogma, the poets of

the Ritikal group, expressed spontaneously and without inhibition, the different aspects of human love and passion, the pangs of separation and the joys of union. It was believed that the poets who mastered the art of writing *sringara kavya* were also masters of all the elements of the *Kama Shastra*. The trend set by the classic, *Gita Govindam*,

❋ *Above:* 'There was a shudder in her whispering voice
She was shy to frame her words
What has happened tonight to lovely Radha?
Now she consents, now she closes up her eyes
Eager to reach the ocean of desire.'

continued well into the 16th century. And while *Gita Govindam* was in Sanskrit, the Ritikal poets wrote in the vernacular: Chandidas in Bengali, Vidyapati in Maithili, Ghananand in Brajaboli (the language of Braj, celebrated as the birth place of Lord Krishna), Keshav Das in Hindi bringing to the people the ideals of erotic sentiment as represented by Krishna and Radha.

Besides the path of faith, purely physical forms of love were also explored. The best known of these was *tantra* that used extreme sexuality to lead, surprisingly, to celibacy. Ancient India believed in the theory of catharsis that once all the deep-rooted emotions and instincts were experienced, spent and thrown out, it would get dissipated and lead to a spiritual quest. Tantra is the one spiritual path that says that sex is sacred, that reaffirms that the coming together of man and woman is worthy of worship and raises sexuality to a spiritual dimension. Tantalizing in its scope with works like the *Yoni Tantra* that is a paean and prayer to the vulva, Tantra has survived to this day as an accepted path that bridges the sacred and the sexual. The word 'tantra' has many definitions, one of which means to weave or hold together. A poetic science of extreme sexuality that dates back over twelve hundred years, it was practised in one form or the other not only in India and Tibet, but also in the Far East and Polynesia.

Besides the physical, the ancients also used the science of yoga and meditation to gain control over the body and mind. Yogic philosophy used several aspects like *asanas* (postures), *pranayama* (breathing) and meditation, because it believed that human happiness and contentment arose from the perfect synchronization between a strong body and a clear mind. Raja yoga as developed by Patanjali around 200 BCE. moved beyond the body and mind and developed a withdrawal of consciousness from the physical world to focus on the inner, spiritual life in a series of eight stages that once again gradually approached the state known as *Sat-Chit-Ananda*.

Numerous paths like *bhakti* or faith, *gyana* or wisdom, texts like the *Kama Shastras,* Tantric works such as the *Kamatantra Kavya* and *Yoni Tantra*, works on Krishna like the *Bhagvatam*, meditation, and yoga, all teach an art that helps explore the hidden dimensions of the unity of the body and the mind, which modern science is only now beginning to understand. All these paths point towards a radically different view about life and sexuality as a means of getting in touch with a higher consciousness. So whatever path one chooses to walk, the final quest shall always remain the search for sublime bliss.

❋ *Facing page:* Tantra reaffirms that the coming together of a man and woman is worthy of worship and raises sexuality to a spiritual dimension.

the pathway of bhakti

human beings in their eternal quest to understand and conceptualize the mysterious creative forces in the world developed a unique concept and called it God. This idea of God, in all religions, was creative, eternal, benevolent, compassionate and all pervasive. The mythologies that grew around this idea were not meant to be taken literally but were metaphorical attempts to describe a reality that was too complex and elusive to express in any other way. Thus while the three major religions of Judaism, Christianity and Islam turned to one absolute God, Hinduism turned to a pantheon—each god was an embodiment of an aspect of the one inexplicable whole.

According to Hinduism, there are as many gods as there are ways to seek the divine and there cannot be any one dogma or one absolute path. The search for spirituality is seen as an individual quest and any path that the individual chooses becomes the right one. Thus there were various ways to seek the divine: the path of *bhakti* (devotion), *dharma* (righteousness), *gyana* (knowledge), *karma* (work), *yoga*, *Tantra* and even *vairagya* (asceticism) Of these the movement that had an immeasurable influence on Indian

literature with its intermingling message of love and worship was the Bhakti movement. Not that the concept of *bhakti* was exclusive to Hinduism, rather it spread through much of South Asia's religions emphasizing the intense emotional attachment and love of a devotee for a personal god. In Buddhism and Jainism, *bhakti* was an infrequent technical term implying veneration and awe of the Buddha and Mahavira respectively. In Islam the rudiments of *bhakti* appeared in works of Sufism and in the veneration of a *pir* or charismatic Sufi figure.

The word '*bhakti*' first makes its appearance in the *Upanishads*, where it is used to explain the concepts of grace and surrender of the self to a Higher Being. Derived from the Sanskrit verbal root '*bhaj*', originally meaning 'to attach, share, to apportion', *bhakti* came to mean 'love, sharing, worship, devotion'. Claiming to be superior because it was open to all—irrespective of gender, class, or caste, the Bhakti movement challenged the dominance of Vedic sacrificial religion, caste boundaries, gender inequity, and the exclusive use of Sanskrit. It thus integrated aspects of personal religious experience, social protest, and a variety of ritual modes that revolved around the central idea of intimacy with one's deity. It thus became a popular folk movement, traceable to the post-Vedic period, though it probably originated earlier among

✺ *Facing page:* In *bhakti* sensuality merges imperceptibly into spirituality where romantic longing breaks out of ethical norms and is no different from the human quest for bliss and ecstasy.

30

the pre-Vedic, pre-Aryan peoples of the Indus reaching its acme during the Middle Ages.

The idea of *bhakti* grew out of the notion that attachment and love operates at various levels, specifically at the material, emotional and spiritual planes. It qualified material love as the attraction for inanimate objects, emotions on the human level as what brought together human beings and on the spiritual level it joined man with God. This last attachment was considered to be most important because as God pervaded everything, he also inhabited the preceding two emotions, the only difference being the channels through which this love was expressed. Worldly love was therefore not considered to be futile as physicality too was seen as an expression of God, gratifying but transient, limited in its scope providing, nonetheless, a path by which love of God could be finally realized. The love for material goods too was accepted though it was considered to be ephemeral because happiness depended on outside factors such as beauty, fame, and fortune. In the quest for happiness and bliss the most gratifying was the association with God. This spiritual love or *bhakti* is directed only to God, whose effulgence puts to shame 'a million suns, a million moons, and a million gods of beauty'.

Bhakti Yoga addressed this need to seek God but recommended ways of worshipping substitutes of God. For instance, the very first scriptural work that expresses the idea of a personal god is the *Bhagavad-Gita* in the epic Mahabharata. 'A devotee "joins his mind with devotion" to a symbol which is not God, taking it to be God.' To identify with this personal God who was endowed with many

✤ Lord Rama symbolizes the Indian ideal of the *Maryadapurushottam*, an exemplary man who embodies the ideal son, husband and brother.

seemingly human attributes became an easier form of seeking the divine—a realistic and acceptable pathway to realizing bliss. Thus it became acceptable to worship God in his various avatars or incarnations, worship his images, chant his name, sing his glory, visit pilgrimage sites, among other things. The medieval Bhakti movement is what was responsible for the many rites and rituals associated with the worship of God by Hindus, Muslims and Sikhs of the subcontinent. The *bhajans* at temples, *qawwalis* at dargahs, the *gurbani* at gurdwaras were devotional songs all derived from the Bhakti movement which sought to serve, honour, revere, love and adore God in any form. The movement spawned several different movements across the country. In the north the cult was essentially based on the Vaishnava sampradaya which rather than focus on the main deity of Vishnu became irrevocably entwined with two of his incarnations: Rama and Krishna, the central characters of the two epics Ramayana and Mahabharata. Adoration of the gods also led to worship of their associated aspects. Thus their consorts also became objects of worship elevating Sita, Rama's wife and Radha, Krishna's companion, though not his wife, into the Hindu religious pantheon.

Bhakti is thus conceptualized as being mystical love for love's sake and can be expressed in different emotions or feelings called *bhavas*. The five main *bhavas* were called *shanta, dasya, sakhya, vatsalya* and *madhurya*. Since these emotions were natural to human beings it was believed that these same feelings could also be used for God. In the *shanta bhava* the devotee is peaceful; in the *sakhya bhava*, God is a friend of the devotee as was Lord Krishna to Arjuna in the Mahabharata. In the *vatsalya bhava,* the devotee looks upon God as a child. The *dasya bhava* stands for submission of a devotee who sees himself as a *dasya* or servant of God. The *madhurya bhava* is the highest form of *bhakti* where the devotee regards the Lord as his or her lover. Although the *madhurya bhava* is completely different from conjugality of the earthly experience, the transformation of the human into the divine was considered to be the beginning of true love for God. *Madhurya* caught the imagination of the nation, and Rama and Krishna became the icons of this emotion.

Among all the Indian deities the ideal man worthy of worship was symbolized by Rama, seen as an upholder of all that was *dharmic* or righteous. The story of his birth, his marriage to Sita, his exile, the abduction of Sita by Ravana the demon king, the ensuing battle leading to the killing of Ravana, and the recovery of Sita continues to captivate the Indian religious psyche and has inspired a body of devotional art, from music, painting, sculpture to poetry and more. In the main text of the Ramayana, there is hardly any mention of *moksha* or salvation, rather *dharma* is considered the most important doctrine and means of attaining a*nanda* or bliss. Rama showed the path by his exemplary conduct as the ideal human being. He was the ideal son, an ideal brother, an ideal husband, Sita his ideal wife, their relationships a representation of the Indian ideal of marriage. Of all the texts on Rama, the one that stands out is Tulsidas's *Ramcharitmanas, (c.* 1574), that portrays Rama as the Absolute Reality while stressing the primacy of *bhakti* and loving devotion to Rama as a personal god.

If Rama represented the ideal man, then

❋ *Facing page:* Rama, the *Maryadapurushottam* in exile, being fed by a devotee.

Krishna was the ultimate *rasik*—the *sringaramurtiman*—the embodiment of the aesthetic experience. Occupying a rather complex place in the Indian narrative tradition, Krishna is variously a mischievous son, a master teacher, a best friend, and not the least, the intimate lover. In this ideal of complete devotion were sown the earliest allusions to *sringara* which is generally understood as the erotic sentiment but more appropriately defined as the feeling of blissful satisfaction while making love. As *kama* or desire came to be acknowledged as the foundation of life, *sringara* come to form the bedrock of the aesthetic experience and, metaphorically, of the mystical experience (see Chapter 3). Thus, not surprisingly, the greatest part of the erotic literature in India deals with Krishna and his consort Radha whose passionate love became sanctified as an expression of *bhakti* where her longing, devotion and love-making becoming worship.

The Bhakti movement was the first and greatest pan-Indian literary and cultural movement spreading across language and regional barriers altering the very fabric of the country's socio-religious sentiment. For example the *Gita Govindam* written in the 12th century comes out of the same socio-cultural milieu that produced the temples at Jagannath Puri and Konarak, as well as those in Khajuraho, whose walls are adorned with erotic sculptures viewed as the sculpted version of the *Kama Sutra*. The years between the 13th and 17th centuries were one of the most prolific, explicit and erotic stages in the development in Indian literature. Ranging from devotional quatrains and *bhakti kavyas*

to court poetry and erotic love songs, this period dealt with a wide range of poetics. Writing without dogma these poets expressed spontaneously and without inhibition the different aspects of human love and passion, the pangs of separation and the joys of union. The development of regional languages meant rejecting the elite tradition of Sanskrit scholarship that had thus far shut out religious texts to the common people. Bhakti also challenged the caste system as many of its poets were from the lower castes. So a common theme of this poetry was that God was within the reach of all human beings irrespective of their caste or creed.

This period saw the rise and dominance of the Mughal rule in the subcontinent. The Hindus, maybe in an attempt to counter the spread of Islam and sensing the need to arouse more devotion among themselves, gave India some of its most sensuous and elegant literature. Written as an expression of love, painted in a variegated palette, in a score of languages, saint-poets like Kabir Das, Guru Nanak, Dharma Das, Maluk Das, Dadudayal, Sunder Das with their *sakhis* (couplets) and *padas* (songs) laid emphasis on the need for the individual to seek the path of God. Besides them there were poets like Chandidas who at the confluence of the 14th and 15th centuries wrote in his native Bengali and is seen today by many as the founder of modern Bengali literature. One of India's best loved poet-saints Surdas's prolific Bhakti poetry was written in Braj bhasha, the language of the region around Mathura as did another poet Bihari (1595-1664), best known for his extremely erotic work called *Satsai*, and *Govindadasa*. All their

✤ *Facing page:* The erotic interplay between Radha and Krishna came to form the bedrock of the aesthetic experience and became sanctified as an expression of *bhakti* where her longing was seen as devotion and their love-making became worship.

compositions had a sensuous simplicity, deriving strength from being based on the local idiom and turn of phrase.

Devotional works, however, did not remain a male domain; there were women writers too. Most often the works by women poets were much more sensuous as they tended to look on God as their lover, making theirs a highly personalized form of worship. Lal Ded (1320-1384) a Muslim poetess from Kashmir wrote in the Sant tradition as did Mirabai (1500 AD) who wrote songs of love and longing for Krishna whom she looked on her as husband:

Come to my bedroom,
I've scattered fresh buds on the couch
perfumed my body
Birth after Birth I am your servant
sleep only with you
Mira's lord does not perish
one glimpse of the Dark One
is all she requests.

Then there was the 12th-century Kannada poetess, rebel and mystic, Akkamahadevi, whose life and writing challenged the patriarchal dominance of the world at large. Said to have wandered naked in search of

❉ Above: 'With some effort
He was able to release himself from my arms
Which firmly held him
And I gently drew my breasts away
So deeply dug into his chest.'

36

divinity, she uses the image of her body to defy her critics. 'Brother, you've come drawn by the beauty of these billowing breasts, this brimming youth. I am no woman brother, no whore.'

As a radical mystic she uses the image of her genitals to convey her understanding of the Bhakti tradition and the Hindu idea of rebirth when she says, 'Not one, not two, not three or four, but through eight four hundred thousand vaginas have I come. I have come through unlikely worlds guzzled on pleasure and pain.'

Another poetess of the Bhakti tradition was Sule Sankavva, whose works often startled contemporary sensibilities with its combination of the sacrosanct and the sacrilegious. Writing as a prostitute, her sentiments about the duplicity of society at large are strongly echoed in her only surviving poem, in which she says: 'In my harlot's trade having taken one man's money, I daren't accept a second man's, Sir. And if I do, they'll stand me naked and kill me, Sir.'

Human emotions and the needs of the body have never escaped anyone. Conquering

✤ Above: 'Let the earth of my body be mixed
With the earth my beloved walks on
Let the fire of my body be the brightness
In the mirror that reflects his face
Let the breath of my body be air
Lapping his tired limbs.'

desire is the mainstay of ascetics who saw it as another pathway to bliss. An interesting tale is often narrated about India's foremost teacher of Advaita philosophy, Adi Shankaracharya, which amply demonstrates that even ascetics of the highest order accepted that every aspect of human emotion had to be explored and experienced, for only then could one successfully transcend it. The stress was on integration and balance; neglecting any area of human emotion would, it was believed, lead to diminished stability and dangerous imbalance. In this narrative, Shankara, the ascetic, was once engaged in a philosophical debate with a Vedic ritualist called Madana

Misra. Bharati, Misra's wife, is said to have engaged Shankara with questions about the erotic arts and sciences. Admitting that true wisdom must include a complete understanding of all aspects of life, the pious celibate asked to be excused from the debate for a month in order to master the theory and practice of love. Shankara, with the help of his magical powers, is believed to have entered the body of Amaru, a king who had died in a hunting accident, to study first hand the dynamics of physical love. Amaru appeared to come back to life and indulged in love games and erotic experiments with his wives and mistresses.

✤ *Above:* 'How soon it's morning already
Have we talked even a little while?
To undo the pain of our separation till now?
Your mouth is still on mine
It's morning already!'

amarushatakam

It is believed that it was Shankara, in the body of Amaru, who wrote this poetic work known as the *Amarushatakam* that displays his mastery of sexual sentiment and the erotic art.

In summer afternoons that are hot and calm
Women anoint their flesh with sandal balm
Lips are red with betel and soft with sighs
As there was mascara from their dark eyes
Clinging robes, hair sweet with floral sprays
How very beautiful women are on such
   summer days

Love had made me dry
So I though I'd try
To quench my thirst, my need
By drinking up the mead
From my lady's lip;
I must have made a slip;
I must have made a slip
My thirst increased by twice
From kisses full of spice.

When my beloved came to bed
My robe slipped loose of its own accord
The skirt barely clung to my thighs
That is all I remember now
Once we touched I could not know who he was
Who I was
Tight-embraces-crushed-breasts-bristling-delight
Intense love swelling feeling girdle skirt slipping
   faint whispers
No
No
Too much
No
Don't
No
Enough

Is she asleep? Is she dead or has she disappeared
   —melted, absorbed into my heart?

The lady's stomach was in knots that night
And her skirt was knotted just as tight.
Angry, she feigned sleep, she turned her face;
Softly he touched the knot—a deft embrace.
So cleverly had these two lovers plotted
That both stomach and skirt became unknotted

In the midst of making love
The girl returned to her senses
Realized what she was doing
She got back her normal defences:
Modesty's a woman's wealth,
Her only source of compensation
Yet my ankles ringing out
Pass on the scandalous information
That I'm a wanton girl!
Thus in the midst of making love
She let go of both her dear man
And her manly posture, up above

Crushed flowers all over the creased and rumpled
   bedcover
Tell the positions in which she made love to her
   lover:
Here smeared with betel juice, juicy and red
(She must have been lying with her face on the bed)
And here there are footprints, her cosmetic lac
(He must have been lying flat on his back)
Here aloe ointments and powder sprays are the clue.

(For position see *Kama Sutra*, Chapter 6: part 2)

❀ 'When my beloved came to bed
My robe slipped loose of its own accord
The skirt barely clung to my thighs
That is all I remember now...'

❉ 'Why do you need a mirror to see
The jewel on your waist?
Some woman has tried to hug you hard
With her hand covered with bracelets...'

tamil anthologies

Tamil tradition tells of three literary academies or *Sangams* that met regularly in the city of Madurai. Nothing survives from the first *Sangam* meeting. Of the second, only texts of early Tamil grammar exist, whilst the works of the poets of the third *Sangam*, the *Ettuthogai* (The Eight Anthologies) and the *Pathu Pattu* (Ten Idylls), form the earliest poems of this extant literature.

Women whose husbands continue unfaithful
though bitterly chided again and again,
   note them flustered, visibly shaken by guilt:
yet, yearning to be loved (in the chill of winter),
   they overlook these wrongs.

Enjoyed long through the long night in love-play
unceasing by their lusty young husbands
in an excess of passion, driving,
   unrelenting, women just stepped into youth
move at the close of night slowly
   reeling wrung-out with aching thighs.

With breasts held tight by pretty bodices,
thighs alluringly veiled by richly dyed silks,
and flowers nestling in their hair,
women serve
   as adornments for this wintry season.

Lovers enjoying the warmth of budding youth,
pressed hard against breasts glowing golden,
saffron-rubbed, of lively women
gleaning sensuous,
sleep, having put to flight the cold.

Young women in gay abandon drink at night
with their fond husbands, the choices wine,
most delicious, exhilarating,
   heightening passion to its pitch:
   the lilies floating in the wine deliciously
   tremble under their fragrant breath.
At dawn, when the rush of passion is spent,
one young woman whose tips of breasts are
   tight

from her husband's embrace, carefully views;
her body fully enjoyed by him
   and laughing gaily, she goes from the bed-
   chamber
   to the living-apartments of the house.

Another loving wife leaves her bed at dawn:
elegant and graceful, slender-waisted,
With deep navel and ample hips;
   the splendid mane of hair with curling ends
flowing loose, the wreath of flowers slips down.

With faces radiant as golden lotuses
   and long, liquid eyes; with lustrous lips
and hair playing enamoured round their
   shoulders,
women shine in their homes these frosty
   mornings,
bearing the semblance of the goddess of beauty.

Young women burdened by their ample loins,
and drooping a little at the waist,
   wearied bearing their own garments worn at
   night
for love's sweet rites,
   they put on others suited to the day.

Staring at the curves of their breasts covered by
   nail marks,
   touching gingerly the tender sprout of the
   lower lip bruised by love-bites,
   young women rejoice to see these coveted
   signs of love's fulfilment,
   and decorate their faces as the sun rises.

It was not in North India alone that the concept of Bhakti flourished. In fact the origins of Bhakti are normally traced to Dravidian religious traditions, where too both Krishna and Shiva got enshrined in erotic devotion. Instead of rejecting desire and power these Bhakti traditions too divinized them by making Shiva or Vishnu the idealized form of the human lover and hero. Bhakti literature in the South largely drew inspiration from the early Sangam literary works that largely explored the sentiment of *aham* (love) and *puram* (heroism). The classical period of Tamil literature known as the Sangam Age is believed to have begun two centuries before the birth of Christ and lasted well into the fourth century. Tamil tradition tells of three literary academies or *Sangams* that met regularly in the city of Madurai. Nothing survives from the first *Sangam* meeting. Of the second, only texts of early Tamil grammar exist, whilst the works of the poets of the third *Sangam*, the *Ettuthogai* (The Eight Anthologies) and the *Pathu Pattu* (Ten Idylls), form the earliest poems of this extant literature. In these formative years, south Indian poems were based either on the subjects of war or love, so its hardly surprisingly, that of the eight anthologies, five deal with love. Most of these poems are permeated by erotic themes and images. The excerpts here (facing page) are mainly from the three anthologies known as the *Kuruntokai*, the *Ainkurunuru* and the *Narrini* that are generally accepted to be the earliest of the Tamil Anthologies.

✤ In the ideal of Krishna bhakti were sown the earliest allusions to *sringara* or the sentiment of eroticism. To this day, Krishna is the embodiment of love, divine and erotic. He is also the philosopher, guide and mentor in the form of Parthasarathy to Partha or Arjun in the *Bhagavad Gita*.

In traditional Tamil poetry, the Krishna of the North becomes Kannan, a playful young man. In Telugu *padams* he is extolled as Muvva Gopala, or the Cowherd of Muvva. Despite its very erotic undertones, this body of poetry is essentially Bhakti poetry as God frequently appears as a lover. These works associated mainly with temples and royal courts in medieval South India, were originally sung and danced to by devadasis or temple dancers and their male counterparts known as Nattuvanar musicians where God assumes the role of a lover as seen through the eyes of his courtesans, mistresses or wives whose persona the poet adopts. The extremely erotic poetry reproduced here is addressed to a personal God and combines an emotional and sensual intensity that is an intrinsic aspect of mystical devotion and erotic discourse which was an integral part of medieval Hindu literature. Despite its very erotic undertones, this body of literature is essentially Bhakti poetry as God frequently appears as a lover. Written in the 15th century in Telugu by the celebrated poet, Ksetrayya, the Muvva Gopala here is the supreme lover, Kama personified. The supremacy of the physical and sensory experience is proclaimed everywhere—for the master of the heart must first be 'Master of my bed.'

❀ *Above:* 'The king of the seasons
Spring has come
And wild with longing
The bee goes to his love.'

44

telugu padams

In Telugu *padams* Krishna is extolled as Muvva Gopala, or the Cowherd of Muvva. Despite its very erotic undertones, this body of poetry is essentially Bhakti poetry as God frequently appears as a lover. These works associated mainly with temples and royal courts in medieval South India, were originally sung and danced to by devadasis or temple dancers and their male counterparts known as Nattuvanar musicians where God assumes the role of a lover as seen through the eyes of his courtesans, mistresses or wives whose persona the poet adopts.

a young woman to a friend

Those women, they deceived me
They told me he was a woman
And now my heart troubles
By what he did.

First I thought
She was my aunt and uncle's daughter
So I bow to her and she blesses me
You'll get married soon
Don't be bashful. I will bring you
The man of your heart.

Those firm little breast of yours
Will soon grow round and full, she says
And she fondles them and starches them
With the edge of her nail
Come eat with us, she says
As she holds me close
And feeds me as at a wedding.

Those women, they told me he was a woman
Then she announces,
'My husband is not in town, come home
   with me.'

So I go and sleep in her bed
After a while, she says
'I'm bored, let's play
A kissing game, shall we?
Too bad we're both women.'
Then, as she sees me falling asleep
Off my guard
She tries some strange things on me
Those women, they told me he was a
   woman
She says, 'I can't sleep
Let's do what men do.'
Thinking, she was a woman,
I get on top of him

Then he doesn't let go
He holds me so tight
He loses himself in me
Wicked as ever, he declares
'I am your Muvva Gopala!
And he touches me expertly
And makes love to me.
Those women, they told me he was a
   woman!

❖ *Following pages 46-47:* The love that bound Radha to Krishna has always been compared to the love of the mystic in search of God who would eventually subsume the mystic's quest.

48

But perhaps the most extraordinary personality in the history of Tamil religious literature is that of Andal, who like her north Indian counterpart Mirabai surrendered her entire life to the devotion of her Lord. Today in Tamil she is known as an *alvar*, one who is 'immersed' in the depths of enjoyment of God. Tradition has it that there were 12 *alvars* of which Andal is the only woman. Travelling from place to place, from temple to temple, from one holy site to another, they composed exceedingly beautiful poetry to their beloved, Vishnu, as an expression of their love for Him.

Andal or Godai was the daughter of a devout brahmin named Vishnuchitta who lived near Madurai. His daily duties included procuring flowers for worship at the local temple. Raised in an atmosphere of love and devotion, her father sang songs to her about God, taught her all the stories and philosophy he knew, and shared his love of Tamil poetry. The love Vishnuchitta had for his Lord intensified in his daughter and before long she was passionately in love with Krishna. She imagined herself to be his bride, playing the role of his beloved, and unknown to her father adorned herself daily with the flower garlands he prepared for the temple. On discovering this, she was promptly warned off by her father. But that night, the Lord appeared to Vishnuchitta in his dream and asked him why he had discarded Godai's garland and that he missed the scent of her body in the flowers. Vishnuchitta awoke with tears of joy suddenly aware of his daughter's intense love; and when she became of marriageable age, the Lord once again appeared in Vishnuchitta's dream and asked that Andal be sent to him in all her wedding finery. On reaching the temple sanctum sanctorum, she embraced the idol of the Lord and merged into him. Andal's works known as *Tiruppavai* transcends the worldly aspects of love and effects the sublimation of the self to merge with God. Andal's love found expression in explicitly poetic but erotic imagery. Experts have speculated on the possible reason for her choice of phrases and believe that as a young girl, on the threshold of womanhood and marriage, it was perhaps natural for her to express her longing for God in terms of sexual fulfilment. The extract below emphasizes a bride's, in this case, Andal's longing for the beloved:

Desire for the Lord consumes me
the Lord who measured the worlds
his power I cannot resist
his slave I have become
the moon and the southern breeze
make me restless and full of sorrow
Do not add to my heartache, O koyil
Do not remain in this grove
Go to Narayana today
Bring him here
Or else I shall drive you away.

She then addresses a song to the dark rain clouds:

O cool clouds
Go to him who churned the ocean deep
Fall at the sacred feet
Of the lotus-eyed Lord

❈ *Facing page:* 'I wait and wait, O clouds rich with water
O clouds bearing lightning within your heart
Tell him who bears the goddess of wealth on His chest
How my young breasts yearn deeply everyday
To clasp his golden chest in tight embrace.'

And make this request on my behalf:
Tell him that my life will be spared
Only if he will come
To stay with me for one day
If he will enter me
So as to leave
The mark of his saffron paste
Upon my breasts.
When in my heart I discover my beloved
When he comes to unite with me
Holding me in close embrace
Will then you rain upon us?

Besides Tamil, the Bhakti tradition was carried on to a number of other languages like Kannada with its medieval poets like Basavanna and Allama Prabhu, Marathi which saw famous poet-saints like Gyaneswar, Eknath and Tuka Ram, where Krishna is venerated in the form of Vitthala or Panduranga.

If Rama and Krishna were iconic representations of the Bhakti movement, the other god of the Trinity, Shiva, was not far behind. The cult of Shiva dates back from the pre-Aryan days to the civilizations of Mohenjodaro and Harappa from which seals of a deity very similar to Shiva known as Rudra were found. Shiva, also known as the erotic ascetic, is to this day worshipped in the form of a phallus throughout the Indian subcontinent. To the minds of the early agriculturists who observed nature, two causes must have struck with force—one the generative power and the other the productive—the active and passive causes. This dual idea must have given rise to comparisons with the mode of reproduction of animals, in which the one was male and the other female. These ideas undoubtedly rose independently and spontaneously in different parts of the world resulting in the almost universal reverence paid to the images of sexual parts now regarded as symbols of the generative and productive principles which in turn became gods and goddesses. Thus the Phallus and the Cteis, the Lingam and the Yoni, could not but become objects of reverence and worship symbolizing the creative energy of all nature. But this worship was never a disinterested or obligatory

🌿 *Above:* 'Shiva!' she cries, 'First among the Gods!' she cries, 'O our father who dwells in Marukal, is it right to afflict this woman with longing?'
Facing page: Nandi, the bull, Shiva's sacred vehicle. Shiva is also worshipped in the form of a *lingam*.

devotion: rather it was a profound and ecstatic though personal worship of God. Here Tirunanacampantar (popularly known as Sambandar or Campantar) one of the earliest and most important of the sixty-three Tamil Nayanars, (Shaivaite leaders) has a rather euphoric devotee in raptures about Lord Shiva:

'Object of my thoughts!' she cries
'Shiva!' she cries
'Primal Being!' she cries
'First among the Gods!' she cries
O our father who dwells in Marukal
where the blue lily blooms in clusters,
is it right
to afflict this woman with longing?

There are numerous erotic tales associated with Shiva but some of the best literature undoubtedly was written by Kalidasa, India's greatest Sanskrit poet and dramatist. Often called India's Shakespeare, his plays *Malavikaagnimitra*, *Vikramorvashiiya*, and *Abhigyaanashaakuntala* are known not just in India but through much of the world. Superbly erotic, his *mahakavya* or epic poem the *Kumarasambhava* describes in great detail the marriage of Shiva to Parvati, their wedding night and the birth of their son Kumara:

'After the wedding ceremony the daughter of the Lord of the Mountains experienced fear mixed with love towards Shiva, but enjoyed the thrilling pleasure that heightened his desire.

'Although she did not reply when addressed, and desired to go away when held by her garment, and slept on the bed with her face turned aside, still she gave delight to Shiva.

'Trembling she obstructed the hand of Sankara as it was placed near the region of her navel, but her garment of its own accord had its knot come completely loose.

'When her lover was before her she came confused and did not remember the advice given by her friends: "O friend in this manner you should wait upon Shiva in private restraining your fear."

'In private, her garments taken off, she closed Shiva's two eyes with her two palms but his third eye in the forehead continued looking her efforts foiled and become helpless.

'Parvati could endure only that and nothing else but on her lover's part, kissing without biting the lower lip, marking with nails without wounding was enjoyment only in moderation.

'Pressed to his bosom, she embraced her lover. She did not turn her face away when he desired her. And she became slack in obstructing his hand as it tremblingly reached to undo her girdle.

'Parvati struck her lover with a golden lotus and had her eyes closed when struck by the spray of water from Shiva's hands; she sported in the River Ganga in the sky, her girdle coming loose by the row of fish that gathered around her waist... .

'Carrying her whose golden girdle was hanging loose and who was heavy on account of the weight of her hips, Shiva entered an abode built of gems and furnished with articles of comfort called into existence by his power of meditation.

'When the night ended even though it was bright daybreak he did not leave the bed, the upper sheets of which had become crumpled into folds, marked by the dye applied to the feet and in the middle of which the girdle with its broken thread lay huddled.'

Yet another manifestation of Shiva equally suffused with eroticism is that of him as the divine androgyne. In Hinduism, the Ultimate Reality is conceived as the union of Shakti (the Divine Feminine) and Shiva (the Divine Masculine); he is *purusha* (spirit), she is *prakriti* (nature), she is *ida*, (subtle female energy), he is *pingala* (subtle male energy); he is the Right-Hand Path, she is the Left-Hand Path. While the ideal of *ardhanarishwara* is that godhood exists without desire it is this whole that became divided into differentiated gender. According to Hindu mythology, it was at the behest of Brahma, and his desire to create beings capable of sexual reproduction, that the Ideal One or *ardhanarishwara* became divided into God and Goddess. It is said that Shiva divided himself and let his Shakti, the body of fire, of which erotic pleasure is the spark, go. The goddess sent her glowing ardour, in the form of a woman, into the world and thus from *ardhanarishwara*'s self-division came the essential idea of woman, sex, and sensuality. The idea of the two principles coming together to become a whole and restoring balance is not exclusive to India but appears in China as the concepts of Yin and Yang. In the Gnostic Gospel of Thomas, Jesus of Nazareth is quoted as having

✳ According to Hindu mythology, it was at the behest of Brahma, and his desire to create beings capable of sexual reproduction, that the Ideal One or *ardhanarishwara* became divided into God and Goddess.

said, 'When you make the two one, and when you make the inner as the outer and the outer as the inner and the above as the below, and when you make the male and female into a single one, so that the male will not be male and the female not be female...then you shall enter the Kingdom of Heaven.'

These archetypes of God as the beloved, lover, or as creative energy was not restricted to Hindu literature or sensibilities. This idea of *bhakti* also found expression as Islamic mysticism or Sufism first arose in Syria and Iraq in the eight century CE, and is believed to derive its name from the Arabic term *suf* or wool for those ascetics who opted out of the worldly race and took to wearing a coarse woollen habit. Although Islam spread rapidly, many converts beneath a veneer of their new faith lived with some of their old beliefs based on asceticism and the need for

an inner life. This quest got transformed into mysticism and the poets who gave vent to this path of realizing God came to be known as Sufi poets. Jayasi, Manjhan, Kutuban and Usman were the pioneers of this school.

One of Sufism's best known exponents, Al-Arabi was born in 1165 CE in Andalusia which was then an outstanding centre of Islamic culture and learning. Prompted by a dream, Al-Arabi began a pilgrimage to the East. His first stop was Mecca where he claims to have received a divine commandment to begin his major work called the *Al-Futuhat al-Makkiyah*. It was also in Mecca that he met Nizam, a gifted and beautiful young woman who—as a living embodiment of eternal wisdom and inspiration to him—is said to have played a role much like that of Beatrice in Dante's

✤ *Above:* As *ardhanarishwara*, Shiva divided himself and let his Shakti, the body of fire, of which erotic pleasure is the spark, go.

life, and for whom Al-Arabi wrote a collection of love poems:

Stay now at the ruins in La`la`i, fading,
and in that wasteland, grieve,
for those we loved.
At the campsite, now abandoned,
stay and call her name,
as your heart is softly torn away.
Everyone who wanted you
you showered with graces.
Only to me did your lightning flash, unfaithful.

Yes, she said, there we used to come
together, in the shade of my branches,
in that luxuriant land.
My lightning was the flash of smiles,
Now it is the blaze of barren stone.
So blame that time
we had no way of warding off.
What fault is it of La`la`i?
I forgave her as I heard her speak,

grieving as I grieved with a wounded heart.
I asked her—when I saw her meadows
now fields of the four scouring, twisting
winds...

Sufi poetry is in equal parts animated by a vision of the Divine as Beautiful, who is synonymous with Truth and Goodness, much like the idea exemplified by the Hindu *Sat-Chit-Ananda*. Many early mystics in Persia are known to have had Hindu teachers and therefore rather like the Bhakti cult, also

gained wide appeal because believers yearned for a god who was personal, more immediate and sympathetic than the remote god of the philosophers and scriptural texts, like the Brahman in Vedic philosophy and the Ulema of Islam. The belief was that each one of us can experience God personally. What was needed was submission, a destruction of the ego and surrender to God.

❋ *Above:* With the waxing moon in the first half of the month, the trigger of love lies in the toe, the foot, the lower back, the knees, the thighs, the navel, the armpits and calves, the cheeks, the throat, the scalp and the lower lip.

Again the Sufi writings of Rabi'a al-'Adawiyya, a woman, for example, runs uncannily parallel to that of the Tamil Andal. Rabi'a is credited as being the first to introduce the theme of love into Sufism—'not just the pious love of God and the brotherly, tranquil love of one's fellow Muslims, but a passionate love whose only goal is unity with God'. In a religion and age where the role of women was anything but positive, where one text was even careful to define Rabi'a as a 'man' before praising her,

how disciples relate to the Buddha, which are clearly suggestive of a Bhakti element in early Buddhism. And their philosophical differences notwithstanding, both Hinduism and Buddhism, recommend the path of devotion as the best means to acquire liberation with desire as an essential motivating factor to achieve the goal. Thus in numerous religious texts, be they Hindu, Christian, Buddhist or Sufi, understanding the underlying principle of unity and balance among all living entities formed the bedrock

and others went so far as to declare women to be created from the sediment of the sins of demons, Rabi'a's name quickly became a synonym for praiseworthy womanhood.

This concept of complete faith, devotion and surrender went beyond narrow religious barriers. Buddhism too, for instance, propagates these very same principles. And although the actual term *'bhakti'* never occurs in the Theravada canon there are aspects of

of the ideal of *bhakti* or spiritual attachment. The coming together of these symbolic concepts of duality as represented by primordial lovers with devotion and complete surrender was seen as a means to attain *ananda* or Supreme Bliss. Reawakening this identity and love was considered to be the ultimate purpose of life and was attainable through the process of Bhakti yoga, the yoga of devotion to God.

❈ *Above:* If a woman is strong, she should be loved
Then in the inverse manner as the site of love changes
So should the mistress be enjoyed.

the Bliss of krishna

hindu mythology is replete with love stories. The very first romance in the recorded history of literature, for instance, comes from India appearing in the Rg Veda (1500 BC). This is the story of Pururavasa (see Chapter 4), a mortal king and his romance with a celestial dancer called Urvashi in the court of Lord Indra. From these hoary, auspicious beginnings, the idea of romance blossomed touching every being, be it a god, king or mortal. Thus there was Vishnu and his consort Lakshmi, the ascetic god Shiva who falls in love and marries the beauteous Parvati, Brahma and Saraswati, kings like Rama and Sita, Nala and Damayanti, Shakuntala and Dushyanta…the list is endless. These were not merely love stories, but rather allegorical representations of the coming together of the male and female elements in nature known as the dual principle of *purusha* and *prakriti*. The entire creation was seen as a manifestation of God where man is *purusha*, the woman *prakriti*, and whose union resulted in *ananda* or bliss. Despite this vast line-up of gods and kings, none of them managed to capture the imagination of a nation as did the incomparable and unique relationship between Radha and Krishna.

Hindu mythology beholds Krishna as the eighth avatar or reincarnation of Vishnu. A dark handsome god, he occupies a rather complex place in the Indian narrative tradition because he has come to mean all things to all people—he is simultaneously a mischievous young child, a trouble-making teenager, an amorous adolescent, a lover beyond compare, a friend, a husband, an advisor, a philosopher, as well as a formidable enemy. The most endearing quality of Krishna is that his was a *poornavatar*—a modern complete man in whom came to rest the disparate elements of human behaviour and emotion. Unlike other philosophies and religions, Krishna celebrated living, playing out life in all its dimensions, accepting and absorbing all of life's contradictions, relationships and indulgences. Recognizing the fact that for desire to be truly fulfilling it has to be a complete experience in which lust and passion were harmonized with emotion and physicality, *sringara* came to form the bedrock of the aesthetic experience and, metaphorically, of the mystical experience too. Thus Krishna, among many other things, became a idealized lover, made to please and pleasure women.

Radha, on the other hand, was the feminine aspect of Krishna, non-differentiated from

🌸 *Facing page:* 'A new Brindaban I see
And renewed barren trees
New flowers are blooming,
And another spring is new
And the sweet boy of Gokul strays
In new and refreshing blossoming ways.'

him; she was *bhava,* pure sentiment, a personification of selfless love that existed entirely for Krishna's pleasure. She is said to be *hladini-shakti,* the bliss potency that resides in Krishna, besides being Krishna's eternal consort and his most faithful devotee. Her passion and uninhibited pursuit of sexual fulfilment with Krishna came to embody every woman's passion, who, abandoning modesty and throwing social decorum to the winds came to seek Krishna's love. With lavish descriptions of the sensuous Radha, with flashing eyes expressing anger at Krishna's infidelities who begs forgiveness for his impetuous dalliances, the Radha–Krishna legend, 'is an evocation of passionate love, an attempt to capture the exciting, fleeting moments of the senses and the baffling ways in which love's pleasures and pains try to regain lost control while editing away love's inevitable confusions'. This symbolic love between Radha and Krishna found expression in the lyrical poetry in all Indian languages. This poetry is echoed in the classical music of great vocalists as well as in the devotional songs of medieval wandering bards who in their rendition sometimes observe and at other times participate in the

✤ *Above:* 'For young the heir of Gokul
And his young passionate mistresses
Meeting new and fresh love-rites
And lights of ever-fresh desire
Sports ever-new delights.'

love play as Krishna's beloved. Immortalized in stone and ink, the bond between the young Krishna and the admittedly older Radha, goes beyond being a mere love affair, becoming the idealized benchmark for every human relationship. Their passionate love came to be sanctified as an expression of *bhakti* seen as the ultimate union, where her love, longing and devotion became worship and his complete sublimation to her was seen as the merging of *purusha* with *prakriti*.

For example, in one of the most famous incidents in the Krishna legend, he steals the clothes of a group of young girls or *gopis* bathing and challenges them to come out of the water thereby revealing themselves. The spiritual interpretation of this incident is believed to be that the one who has faith and is a firm believer must completely surrender oneself to the divine forces.

Thus Radha herself says:

All my inhibition left me in a flash,
when he robbed me off my clothes,
but his body became my new dress.
Like a bee hovering on a lotus leaf
He was there in my night, on me! True,
the god of love never hesitates!
He is free and determined like a bird
winging toward the clouds it loves.
Yet I remember the mad tricks he played,
my heart restlessly burning with desire
was yet filled with fear!

In Vedic literature, the Absolute Truth is described as *Sat-Chit-Ananda Vigraha*, which means the personal form of eternal knowledge and bliss. Since God, also known as Brahman or the Supreme Consciousness, was seen as being unchanging, dormant and non-responsive, something one could not have a personal relationship with, the personal form of Krishna came to embody the dynamics of spiritual bliss, in whom *ananda* came to be ever present, expanding and growing to cover all dimensions of human emotions. The most sublime experience of this spiritual bliss is called *rasa,* in which Krishna is the taste, centre and source of all ecstatic experiences. The consummation of Krishna's love affair with Radha, in which he himself bows to her love is best described in five chapters of the *Bhagavata Purana*'s tenth canto. Many consider the *rasa-lila* to be the most erotic and sensuous tale ever written.

The *Puranas* play a very important role in the popular religious expressions of Hindu India. Regarded as sacred works they are a collection of laws, tales, and a philosophy that reflect the teachings of older scriptures. Of these the *Bhagavata Purana* as well as the *Brahmavaivarta Purana*, written around the 10th century AD are books dedicated to Krishna and his *rasa-lila* with Radha and the cowherd girls known as *gopis*.

❀ The personal form of Krishna came to embody the dynamics of spiritual bliss, in whom *ananda* came to be ever present, expanding and growing to cover all dimensions of human emotions.

❋ 'Mirror in hand she appears now
And asks of her sweet girl-comrades to show
What love is and what love does
And all shamed delight that sweet love owes.
And often she sits by herself and sees
Smiling with bliss her breasts increase.'

❊ 'In the spring moonlight the Lord of Love
The crown of love's raptures proves
For Radha his amorous darling moves
Radha, the ruby of ravishing girls
With him bathed in love's moonlight whirls
And all the merry maidens with rapture.'

lord krishna's dalliance
with the *gopis*

The eminent Suka said:

'When the *gopis* heard the charming, well-phrased words of the Blessed Lord, they left behind them the suffering which had resulted from separation, and their desires were both strengthened and satisfied by touching the limbs of His body.'

Then and there Govinda, surrounded by those jewels of women—so devoted to Him and so joyful—started the *rasa*-game, as the *gopis* linked their arms together.

The joyous festivity of the *rasa*-dance, embellished by the circle of *gopis*, was fully set in motion by Krishna, the Lord of Yoga, who entered the circle between the two members of each pair of *gopis*, and put one arm around the neck of each *gopi*, so that all these women would think that He was in her presence alone. Meanwhile the sky all around was crowded with a hundred heavenly chariots, containing the sky-dwellers (*i.e.*, gods) and their wives, both of whose very selves had been carried away by ardent desire.

Then the booming of the kettledrums began, and flowers rained down, as the Gandharva husbands, accompanied by their wives, sang in praise of the untainted Fame of Krishna.

A noisy confusion of sound came from the bracelets, anklets and tiny bells of these women as they danced with their Lover in the *rasa*-circle. In that dance the Blessed Lord, Devaki's son, shone with surpassing brilliance together with the *gopis*, like an emerald set in the midst of gold ornaments.

With the movements of their feet and the waving of their arms, the coquettish arching of their eyebrows accompanied by smiles, and the bending of their waists, the shake and bouncing of their breast-cloths, and with the swaying of their earrings against their own and His cheeks, these brides of Krishna, their faces perspiring and the knots of their braids and girdles come loose, now sang in praise of Him as they flashed brilliantly, like bolts of lightning in a circle of black clouds.

The sweet voiced *gopis* in love with love sang out in high-pitched voices as they danced. And as they were delighted by the touches of Krishna, their song pervaded this world. One *gopi* intoned together with Mukunda, the Pure, unmixed types of notes

and she was honoured by him as He showed his love for her saying, 'Well done! Well done!'

One *gopi* exhausted from the *rasa*-dance hung on with her arm to the shoulder of the club wielder (Krishna) who was beside her as the jasmine flower-braided bracelet in her hair shook loose. Another *gopi* was dancing and singing, her ankle bells and waist bells jiggling. And exhausted, she placed the blessed lotus

❊ 'When, again and again bathing in Yamuna's waters
Muddied with the musk that had anointed Her breasts,
I search for my queen in Vrindavana's charming forest groves,
And call, "O Radha, do you not see the path Your playful lover took?" '

hand of Achyuta who was beside her on her breasts. The *gopis* having gained for themselves a lover who never fails or tires, Achyuta who is the one and only beloved of Sri, sang his praises as he put his arms around their necks and they played.

The *gopis*, their faces glowing radiantly with perspiration and their cheeks adorned by the tips of the curls that looped round the blue lotus blossoms in their ears and with the ringing of their bracelets and anklets providing instrumental music, danced together with the Blessed Lord, their garlands having fallen from their hair, in the partnership of the *rasa*-dance while the bees filled the roles of the singers.

63

Thus, with embraces and with touches of His hands, with loving glances, unrestrained love-play and with laughter, the Lord of Rama enjoyed the delights of love with the beautiful women of Vraja, just as a little boy plays delightedly with his own mirrored image.

Their senses overwhelmed by the ecstasy of touching His body, the women of Vraja were not able to rearrange quickly their hair, their woven-silk dresses, or their breast-cloths, or, O best of the Kuru race, their garlands and ornaments, which slipped off. When they saw this special game played by Krishna, the wives of the gods were dazed, wounded by passion, and the half-marked moon, with his host of stars, was awestruck.

After multiplying Himself so that there were as many forms of Him as there were cowherd-women, this Blessed Lord made love with these *gopis*, even though His delight is in Himself, playfully—as a game. The *gopis* were exhausted by this excess of love-play, and He, compassionate, wiped their faces lovingly, good sir, with His most blessed hand.

The *gopis*—with their flashing gold earrings, their lustrous hair, and the radiance of their cheeks, and with His laughing glance, like the nectar of the gods—honouring their virile Lover, sang in praise of the sacred works He had done, filled with joy by the touch of His fingernails.

Accompanied by the *gopis*, and pursued by bees, the protector-Gandharvas of His garland, which was now coloured with saffron-paste from the *gopis'* breasts and crushed by the contact with their bodies, the Lord, exhausted, entered the river's waters to remove the fatigue of all, just as a weary bull-elephant plunges into the water with his female-elephants, after breaking the dam.

He and they were now fully in the water as these girls splashed Him, and they looked at Him with love as their loud laughter flowed in on Him from all sides, O Dear One. He was praised by the gods, who rained down flowers from their heavenly chariots, and He made love in whatever way He wished—since His love here is the game of the bull-elephant.

After this, the Lord surrounded by the swarms of love-crazed *gopis* and bees—just like a tusker, his rut-fluid streaming, with his female elephants—went into the little grove on the black Yamuna, a grove swept pleasantly in all its shady reaches by the breeze which bore the fragrance of the blossoms of land and water. And so the Lord, accompanied by this flock of women so fond of Him and so truthful and fulfilled in their desires, and confining His seed firmly within Himself, passed joyfully all these brightened-by-moonbeam nights, whose tales are told in the poetry of autumn and which are the refuge of the mood of the season.

❊ *Facing page:* 'When her friends had gone
Smiles spread on Radha's lips
Seeing the mood in Radha's heart
Hari spoke to his love
From his bed of buds and tender shoots.'

✳ 'Her passion rose when glances
played on his seductive face
Like an autumn pond when
wagtails mate in lotus blossom
hollows
She saw his passion reach the soul
of Hari's mood
The weight of joy strained his face;
Love's ghost haunted him.'

himself into two parts. The right side of his body became Krishna, the left side became Radha. The

round her waist was constructed with gems. Then Radha went to a desirable place at a distance and

lovely Radha in the sphere of the *rasa* too wanted intercourse with Krishna… the jovial Krishna was excited with lust at the sight of his young licentious spouse who was bending under the pressure of her huge buttocks. She ran to her husband when she saw that he was excited with passion.

It is on that circular dancing ground that Krishna decked with a yellow dress and ornaments of gem, besmeared with sandal paste and adorned with wreaths of pearls sported with the *gopis* in their endlessly ecstatic dance. And there the eternal Radha, the mistress of the *rasa* always serves Lord Krishna. …The charms of her

excited with passion, clasped and kissed him again and again with a thrill of raptures.

Radha was excited with lust and a thrill of rapture animated her frame. She went to the sleeping room and applied the paste of aloe and sandal mixed with musk and saffron to the chest of Lord Krishna. Then Lord Krishna held Radha by the hand, embraced and kissed her and loosened the cloth that covered her body. O Saint, in this

❋ *Above:* 'Glory to the Forest-Goddess
When, wounded by millions of Kamadeva's arrows
Nanda's son fell.
She brought Him to life by splashing Him with many waves of
The blissful nectar of Her touch.'

war of love, the small bell worn by Radha as an ornament was torn from her body: the hue of her lips was removed by kisses: the paintings with cosmetics were wiped out by Krishna's embraces, the hair was dislocated, the mark of vermilion was obliterated by sexual intercourse and the lac-dye paintings on her feet removed by sexual intercourse performed in the reverse order. There was a thrill of rapture in her body owing to the excitement—she nearly lost her reason and could not distinguish night from day.

Then the most witty Hari committed with her the eight kinds of sexual intercourse systematically

the same time and entering into every chamber committed sexual intercourse with each and every woman in the lovely sphere of the *rasa*. In his intercourse with nine lakh milkmaids, he assumed nine lakh forms of cowherds…. The ornaments of everyone were shattered. That place solely resounded with the noise caused by armlets, bracelets and anklets. The passionate Krishna in the first place sprinkled Radha's body with water. Radha also poured three handfuls of water on the body of the passionate Krishna. Then Krishna snatched away the clothes of Radha, tore off her flower garlands and treated her with such

assailed her with teeth, nails and hands and kissed her in eight mysterious ways consistent with the doctrine of sexual science and delightful to the ladies…. At the time of sexual intercourse the passionate Hari with the different members of the body embraced delightfully the different members of the bodies of the lustful damsels…so that war of love knew no intermission. Thus the lord of Radha assumed identical forms at one and

✻ *Above:* 'My thoughts rest in the name Radha
The essence of beauty, the essence of nectar
The essence of happiness, the essence of mercy
The essence of playful amorous pastimes
The essence of the best of everything.'

urgency in the water that the wonderful hue of her lips and the linings of her eyes with collyrium were all obliterated by its churning… .

In the thirty-three forests the *gopis* passionately sported for thirty-three days and yet their desire was not satisfied. Their passion instead of being satiated increased like fire fed with clarified butter. The gods and goddesses were very much astonished at the sight of repeated sexual intercourse… .

✻ *Following pages 70-71:* Krishna, the divine lover, often frolicked with the *gopis* or cowherd girls, stealing their clothes when they went for a dip in the river.

69

ागीतगोविंदरोएछाःप्पाः धरसुधाःश्रीकल्लराधिकाप्रतिकेकरैाहेमं
लिक्षःआदासबीनंडींवलेककिसोकुंःविलासकरेरहिताविरलानकरे

Gita Govindam

In the *Gita Govindam*, in wondrous post-coital bliss, Radha commands Krishna to paint her feet, comb her tresses, and in general do whatever she commands.

His body hair bristled to the art of her sensual play
Gleaming jewels ornamented his graceful form
She saw his passion reach the soul of Hari's mood
The weight of joy strained his face; Love's ghost
    haunted him.

Her eyes transgressed their bounds
Straining to reach beyond her ears
They fell on him with trembling pupils
When Radha's eyes met her lover
Heavy tears of joy
Fell like streaming sweat.

She neared the edge of his bed
Masking her smile by pretending to scratch
As her friends swarmed outside
When she saw her lover's face
Graced by arrows of love,
Even Radha's modesty left in shame
But driven by love's fever
Radha rode over her lover
Trying to dominate him
Nevertheless, her hips slowed down,
Arms grew slack,
her heart beat fast, and her eyes were closed.
How can women attain the prowess of men?

Throbbing breasts aching for loving embrace are
    hard to touch,
Rest these vessels on my chest! Quench love's
    burning fire!
Narayana is faithful now. Love me Radhika!

Offer your lips' nectar to revive a dying slave,
    Radha!
His obsessed mind and listless body burn in love's
    desolation.
Narayana is faithful now. Love me Radhika!

Displaying her passion
In love play as the battle began
She launched a bold offensive
Above him
And triumphed over her lover.
Her hips were still,
Her vine-like arm was slack,
Her chest was heaving,
Her eyes were closed,
Why does a mood of manly force
Succeed for women in love?

Then, as he idled after passionate love,
Radha, wanting him to ornament her,
Freely told her lover,
Secure in her power over him,
'Yadava Hero, your hand is cooler than sandal
    balm on my breast;
Paint a leaf design with deer musk here on
    love's ritual vessel!'
She told the joyful hero, playing to delight her
    heart!

'My beautiful loins are deep caverns to take the
    thrust of love—
Cover them with jewelled girdles, cloths, and
    ornaments, Krishan!'
She told the joyful hero, playing to delight her
    heart!

'Paint a leaf on my breast
Put colour on my cheeks!
Lay a girdle on my hips
Twine my heavy braid with flowers!
Fix rows of bangles on my hands
And jewelled anklets on my feet.'
Her yellow-robed lover
Did what Radha said…

Significant if not central to the Radha-Krishna relationship is the fact that women were given a role of near equality when it came to the pursuit of erotic pleasure. Even before the 3rd century, when Vatsyayana is believed to have compiled the *Kama Sutra*, women sought and were indeed encouraged to seek their fulfilment without fear or favour. Indeed the ongoing debate on the relationship between Radha and Krishna, whether she was older than him, whether she was *svakiya*, his wife, or *parakiya*, another man's wife, comes to naught when faced with the degree of ecstasy that was derived from this love. This sensitivity to the needs and feelings of women is portrayed beautifully in the *Gita Govindam*, when, in the last canto, in the wondrous languor of post-coital bliss, Radha commands Krishna to paint her feet, comb her tresses, and in general do whatever she commands. In fact, the emergence of Radha as Rasheshvari, the very embodiment of the mood of *sringara*, takes the erotic theme far beyond the plaintive desire of the besotted *gopis* of the *Bhagvata Purana*.

The new heroine in Krishna's love is a compellingly striking woman: beautiful, aloof, proud, sensitive, brooding, willful and passionate. And no one has described it better than Jayadeva for whom love was not just a metaphor for devotion, but it also existed in its own right as a path to the divine. The *Gita Govindam* is a poem that extols the physical love between Krishna and Radha without any reservation or apology and is even today sung as a hymn in temples. These deceptively simple verses earned sainthood for its writer whose ascetic life came to an end when a Brahman in Puri insisted that Lord Jagannath himself had ordained a marriage between Jayadeva and the Brahman's daughter, Padmavati a dancer dedicated to the temple. It is said that as Jayadeva composed, she danced and the outcome was the *Gita Govindam*. An interesting legend is associated with the writing of the 10th canto of this magnificent poem. Hesitating to write out the climax, in which he had Radha place her foot on Krishna's head in a symbolic gesture of victory, Jayadeva apparently went to the river to bathe. It is said that in his absence, Krishna himself appeared to complete the couplet. When Jayadeva returned, he realized that he had received divine grace in exalting Krishna's love for Radha. The *Gita Govindam* reaches the acme of the sublime love between a man and a woman. Replete with lyrical religious eroticisms, its 12 cantos ushered in a new era in Indian literature, with an impact like a tidal wave. Within a century or two of its writing, its explicitly erotic verse acquired unprecedented popularity all over India, particularly in Bengal. From the 14th to the 16th century, a host of poets carried forward the legacy of Jayadeva and the conflation of the Radha-Krishna myths became profoundly influential.

✳ Krishna's love is a compelling, striking woman...

73

Inspired by both the Bhakti movement as well as the overtly expressive *Gita Govindam* the lovers Radha and Krishna assumed cult status. The flowering of their cult gave rise to not just the erotic mystical Vaishnavite cults of Chaitanya Mahaprabhu in Bengal and Vallabhacharya in Mathura but also influenced Rajasthani and Pahari miniature painters: in these works Radha is often seen either waiting for Krishna to return with the cows at twilight, or sitting with him in a bower engaged in amorous play. More importantly the Radha-Krishna cult gave birth to the most refined and productive stages in the development of Indian literature. Following the Bhaktikal or devotional period that saw an outpouring of *bhakti kavyas* or devotional poems, was the Ritikal period that expressed spontaneously and without inhibition, different aspects of human love and passion— from the pangs of separation to the joys of union. The concepts of *alankara* (ornamentation) and *sringara* almost defy description but represent in essence beauty, sensuality and a highly refined sense of aesthetics. The ultimate *rasiks* or connoisseurs of the *sringara rasa* became Radha and Krishna, who after the *Gita Govindam* gained immense popularity. Writing without dogma the poets of the Ritikal group wrote in the vernacular bringing to the people the ideals of erotic sentiment as epitomized by Krishna and Radha.

The best known among these Ritikal poets is Vidyapati who wrote a collection of 900 songs centred on Radha. Writing in the well-known tradition of the *Kama Sutra* and influenced by Jayadeva, Vidyapati's love songs concentrate on the intense passion of Radha's love. At once sensuous and sensual, descriptive and dramatic, Vidyapati's songs go way beyond rhyme and metre, finding their place in the human heart. Vidyapati's works stand out since in his works, God is the supplicant, playing a submissive role as he worships his woman Radha.

'For heaven's sake, listen, listen, O My Darling: Do not dart your cruel, angry glances at me, For I swear by the lovely pitchers of your breasts, And by your golden, glittering, snake-like necklace: If ever on earth I dare touch anyone except you, Let your necklace turn into a real snake, and bite me; And if ever my promise and words prove false, Chastise me, O Darling, in the way you want to. But, now, don't hesitate to take me in your arms, Bind, bind my thirsty body with yours; bruise me with your thighs, and bite, bite me with your teeth. Let your fingernails dig deep, deep into my skin! Strangle me, for heaven's sake, with your breasts, And lock me in the prison of your body forever!'

✳ Krishna as the ultimate *rasik* or connoisseur of the *sringara rasa*.

vaishnava padaval

Vidyapati's best-known work called the *Vaishnava Padaval* is a collection of 900 songs centred on Radha, and although eroticism was common in medieval Sanskrit literature, Vidyapati brought into the vernacular the boldness and sensuality of the early Sanskrit texts.

His language is powerful, often violent, to express the power of the union between the worshipper and God, between a man and a woman.

all my inhibitions

All my inhibitions left me in a flash,
When he robbed me of my clothes,
But his body became my new dress.
Like a bee hovering on a lotus leaf,
He was there in my night, on me.

first rapture

There was a shudder in her whispering voice.
She was shy to frame her words.
What has happened tonight to lovely Radha?
Now she consents, now she closes up her eyes,
Eager to reach the ocean of desire.
He begs her for a kiss.
She turns her mouth lily, the moon seized her.
She felt his touch startling her girdle.
She knew her love treasure was being robbed.
With her dress she covered up her breasts.
The treasure was left uncovered.
Vidyapati wonders at the neglected bed.
Lovers are busy in each other's arms.

fear and love

O Friend, Friend, take me with you.
I am only a young girl,
No one can stop him
So violent a lover is he.

My heart shudders to go near him.
How the black-bee ravishes the lotus-bud.
For hours,
He crushes my frail body
Quivering like a drop of water
On a lotus leaf.
How long must I endure the curse of life?
Which god invented that she-demon night?
Vidyapati says: Who can believe you?
Do you not see that dawn in coming?

torment

O Friend, how can I say what happened in the night?
Madhava was torture.
Thrusting his fingers on my breasts
He drank my lips.
Pressing his face hard on mine,
He took my life away.
His youthful strength
So wantonly aroused
Drugged his senses.
A country boy,
He did not know
The art of love.
I prayed and begged in vain.
Vidyapati says: My dear lady,
You are enchanted by that greedy god.

sacred moon

I cannot guess your heart,
O Madhava!
The treasures of another man
I offered to you:

Facing page: The idea of *bhakti* is one of surrender and variously
means love, sharing, worship, devotion and renunciation.

❀ Meanwhile rapture-
waking string
Ripest of strains the sonata
of spring
That lover and lord of love-
languid notes
With tired delight in
throbbing throats.
And rumours of violin and
bow
And the mighty Queen's-harp
mingle and flow.

I was wrong
To bring a she-elephant to a lion.
Relinquish then the wife of another.
Your kisses have wiped clean
The mascara of her eyes.
Her lips are torn by your teeth.
Her full-grown breasts
Are scarred by your nails:
The autumn moon is scratched by Siva's peak…
Mountains of Gold
In joyous words he spoke
Of the beauty of my face.
Thrilled, my body
Glowed and glowed.
My eyes that watched love spring
Were wet with joy.
In dream tonight
I met the king of honey…
He seized the end of my dress,
The strings broke loose
With all the weight of love.
My hands leapt to my breasts
But the petals of lotus could not hide
The mountains of gold.

ecstacy

Her hair, dishevelled,
Veils the beauty of her face
As evil shadows eat the glowing moon.
Strings of blossom in her hair
Wantonly play
As flooded rivers
Twine about their twins.
Exquisite today,
This sport of love,
As Radha rides on Krishna.
Beads of sweat glisten on her face
Like pearls on the moon,
A present to her
From the God of Love.

With all her force
She kisses her lover's lips,
Like the moon swooping
To drink a lotus bloom.
Her necklace dangles
Below her hanging breasts,
Like streams of milk
Trickling from golden jars.
The jingling bells around her waist
All I want is to sleep
Krishna makes love
The whole night through,
Like a bee that lingers
On the fragrant Malati.
He sucks my lips.
The forest has burst open
With white *kunda* blooms,
But the bee is enraptured
By Malati and her honey.

new love

The style of the new moon, stirrings of new love,
Scratches of nails scarring her firm breasts.
At times she eyes them and at times she shields,
As poor hands cover treasure dear as life.
For the first time she knew the act of love.
The joys of dalliance fill her thoughts,
Wrapping her round with shuddering of delight.
Safe from the eyes of vicious friends,
She holds a gem as mirror to her face,
Lowers her brow that none can see
And then with tender care
Studies the love-bites on her lower lip.

॥सखिमोहतगोपालकेउरगुंजनकीमालाबाहिरलसतमनोपियेंदावा
नलकीझालाॸ६ॸ॥

❊ 'At the third watch of the night
I was clasped to his heart
Still gazing at his moonlike face
Smiling, he stole my heart away.'

अधरभरत हरिकेपरत ओठ दीठिपरज्याति हरितबांसकीबांसुरीइंद्रधनु
रंगहोति ॥१३॥

❀ 'O sweet is Brindaban today
And sweeter than these our Lord of May
His maiden-train the sweets of earth
Honey-girls with laughter and mirth
Sports of love and dear delight.'

aftermath

Your eyes droop with sleep
Yet still your face
Outshines the lotus.
Who was that fool
Who scarred your breasts,
Marring their god-like charms
With savage nails? Your brow no longer wears
Its mark of scarlet.
Your lips of coral
Are drained grey.
Who has raided, my love,
Your house of treasure?

in ecstacy

In ecstasy I closed my ears
And then the God of Love
Lifted his bow
And sprayed me with his arrows.
My body was borne away
By the dew of my skin.
My make-up was afloat.
Trembling with delight,
My breasts burst from my bodice
And my bracelets were in pieces.
Beloved in passion,
Who shared the joys of love with you?
Your secret is out, why are you so shy?
His forces of love
The god has roused in you.
Your thighs tremble.
The golden skin of your breasts
Is scarlet from his nails
Yet still you try to hide them.
Radha, you are an ocean of nectar
And Krishna is afloat in it
Like a furious elephant.
Who was that girl?

Friend, who was that girl
Inflaming the river
With her fair skin?…

a bending lotus

Suddenly her dress slipped,
And she covered her breasts with her hands,
As if two lotuses and ten moons
Covered the golden Plahhus
How shall I explain?
My heart became restless
And eyes went out of sorts,
During her glances smilingly,
She bent her head—
And the age passed,
But to see the beauty of a bending lotus.

Lend your ears
To these profitable words
O beautiful girl
Great is the virtue
Of serving others
She who never encounters
Rapture outside marriage
May her face stay
Away from my path
A girl who is unaware of
The happiness of love
With at least five men
Is as unholy
As an evil spirit
Says Vidyapati:
Listen my girl of great merit,
A woman of one husband
Knows nothing of love.

Vidyapati was followed by Chandidas whose songs still resound in the rural areas of West Bengal where, to this day, at night people gather in temple courtyards or in the village greens to listen to professional singers sing his songs of the divine love of Radha and Krishna. Chandidas was a votary of the Sahaj movement or the Sahajiya cult which believed that in sexual love one could find a higher meaning that pointed to divine love. His *padavalis* or works left a deep impact on Bengal literature which can be glimpsed in the works of Rabindranath Tagore, Govind Das and others:

> Chandidas says with a joyful heart,
> Suffering leads to the treasures of love.
> Consuming me, she moved away,
> The golden goddess.
> The glow of her skin ripped open her sari
> As her form fought with the azure blue dress.
> How would I hold
> The lightning in my eyes?—
> I could no longer watch.
> Her eyes were restless,
> Bracelets jingled...

> The first watch of the night was a world of a lovely dream!
> Under the Kadamba tree Kanu held me to his side,
> Kissed my lotus-like face.
> Painting me with sandal paste, gently he spoke to me
> And sweetly played on his bamboo flute.
> He wanted to make love to me,
> But I did not let him.
> I was still dreaming till the second watch.
>
> At the third watch of the night I was clasped to his heart,
> Still gazing at his moon-like face.
> Smiling, he stole my heart away,
> I was anxious and restless for love.
> At the fourth watch of the night Kanu drank my lips,
> And I longed to be loved. Sings Babu Chandidas:
> Suddenly a cruel scream from the morning *kokila* bird
> Shattered me and my dream.

> My poor darling
> Your face seems hollow

It hurts me to see
You adorned this way
Your forehead, alas
Is bruised by bracelets
She must be wild
Who did this to you?
Your chest looks furrowed
With finger nail scares
Like red lotus blooms
On a clear blue pool
Who is that stone girl?
That harbours such ways
Whoever taught her?
This kind of loving
It hurts me to see
Your eyes so damp
Sit by me, Darling,
I'll wipe your face clean
You must be tired
Of the sleepless night.

I must go
Inspire of my kisses
My passionate embraces
He keeps repeating
That he must go
He goes half a step
And then he turns back
With anguished eyes
Gazing at my face.

Wringing my hands
He promises returning
He flatters me so much
To meet me again
Deep is his love
My beloved one
Of such terrible passion
Chandidas says, then
Rest in his heart.

❋ 'With him bathed in moonlight's whirls
And all the merry maidens with rapture
Dancing together the light winds capture
Meanwhile rapture—waking string
Ripest of strains the sonata of spring...'

✽ 'I always sing Radha's name
In the forest with my flute
And I always meditate on Her
Covered as she is with goose pimples of ecstasy...'

Arguably the most erotic of the Radha-Krishna literature emerged from the Bengali Sahajiya movement which can be traced back long before Sri Chaitanya Mahaprabhu's appearance, to the reign of the Buddhist Pala royal dynasty (*c.* 700-1100 AD), when a secret cult of the name Sahajayana arose within the so-called Vajrayana (Diamond Vehicle) school of Buddhism. Sahajayana Buddhists abandoned ritualism and the study of scriptures as useless. They practised a yoga of sex in which they visualized consciousness as being composed of the unity of the male and female principles. Sahajayana Buddhists wrote many songs known as the *Caryapadas* that expressed their philosophy that was clothed in mysticism. Later on when Vaishnavism was on the rise in Bengal, Sahajayna Buddhists absorbed aspects of Vaishnava philosophy giving rise to Gaudiya Vashnavisim where the term 'Gaudiya' means 'of *Gauda-desa*', *Gauda-desa* being an old name for West Bengal. This widespread Bhakti movement was begun by Chaitanya Mahaprabhu in the late 15th century and he is generally accepted by all his disciples to be an incarnation of Krishna. His disciples called Goswamis renamed the male and female principles 'Krishna' and 'Radha', imagining Radha and Krishna to represent the highest state of bliss attained by a man and a woman. Using the Radha-Krishna relationship as a means to examine the issue of eroticism and sexuality in the human-divine love relationship where passionate love gets sanctified as an expression of *bhakti*, the Goswamis, including Rupa Goswami, Sanatana Goswami, Sri Krishnadasa Kaviraja and others wrote exquisite and often erotic poems.

The excerpts here are from Krishnadasa Kaviraja's *magnum opus, Sri Chaitanya-Charitamrta*, Vishvanatha Chakravartin's *Krishna-bhavanamrta* and Prabodhananda Sarasvati's *Ascharya Rasa Prabandha*.

Sri Krishnadasa Kaviraja Goswami was born in 1496 in a family of Ayurvedic physicians called *kavirajas,* and is believed to have been instructed in a dream to go to Vrindavana, where 'all things could be attained'. He then renounced the world and took shelter with the Goswamis in Vrindavana where he wrote the *Sri Chaitanya-Charitamrta*, a definitive biography of Chaitanya Mahaprabhu. Besides this biography, he also wrote the *Govinda-lilamrta* as well as the *Krishna-karnamrta*, both works that examine the whole cycle of playful interactions that are believed to take place between Radha and Krishna in an eternally recurring cycle of day and night in their world, Gokula.

Shri Chaitanya-Charitamrta

S ri Krishnadasa Kaviraja Goswami was born in 1496 in a family of Ayurvedic physicians called *kavirajas,* and is believed to have been instructed in a dream to go to Vrindavana, where 'all things could be attained'. He then renounced the world and took shelter with the Goswamis in Vrindavana where he wrote the *Sri Chaitanya-Charitamrta*, a definitive biography of Chaitanya Mahaprabhu.

O Sakhi, see the delight of Krishna's water-
   sport!
Krishna the mad rut-elephant,
His hands the restless tips of the trunk,
With the *gopis*, the cow-elephants.

They begin the water-play,
throwing water at one another,
and in the scuffle showers of water rain
   down.
All conquer and are conquered, nothing is
   certain,
and the water-fight escalates endlessly.

At first the fight was throwing water,
then it became hand-to-hand warfare,
and then mouth-to-mouth.
Then the war went breast-to-breast,
then tooth-to-tooth,
then the war shifted to nail-to-nail.

They kissed him with a thousand lips,
embraced him with a thousand bodies,
and listened to his jokes with a thousand
   ears.

Krishna took Radha forcefully
And went neck-deep into the water,
And released her there where the water was
   deep

There she hung on the neck of Krishna
And floated on the water
Like a lotus uprooted by an elephant.

All the *sakhis*, like lotus-creepers,
Gave them help,
And with hands like waves presented them with
   leaves,
Some with strands of loosened hair
Covered their lower parts,
And covered their breasts with their hands.

Now Krishna with Radha
Did what was in his mind
And went to search for the *gopis*
And Radha who was of subtle mind
Knowing where the *sakhis* were,
Came and mingled with them.

Krishna was most delighted
And sat down to the forest feast
With her companions
Radha then ate,
And the pair lay down in the temple.
Some fanned them
And some massaged their feet
And some fed them t*ambula*;
Radha and Krishna slept,
And the *sakhis* lay down
And watching this my heart was pleased.

❋ 'When Radha's name enters My ears
I don't know who I am, where I am
Where I came from
Or what I am going to do...'

✳ 'Who can properly praise this flute that rests on Kanhaiya's lips
That which destroys the pride of all the *gopis*?
Which beautiful *gopi* can remain calm after hearing its sound
Which causes their blouses and girdles to fall off?'

krishna-bhavanamrta

In the two texts that follow, the erotic encounters of Radha and Krishna are seen as part of a visualization practice. The practitioner develops a new identity, usually that of a thirteen-year-old girl called a *manjari* who is a servant or *sakhi* of one of the chief friends of Radha (like Visakha or Lalita). These *manjaris* as servants get to stay close to Radha and Krishna during their intimate moments, fanning them or playing music or offering them betel, among other things. It is from this voyeuristic vantage point that they witness the intimacies of Krishna and his lady. The first is from Vishvanatha Chakravartin's work called *Krishna-bhavanamrta*, where he watches the various stages of a day in the life of Radha and Krishna as though he were Radha's handmaiden.

chapter one

enjoying the sport of rising from bed

I surrender to the rain-cloud Krishna Chaitanya, who destroys the phenomena of darkness and refreshes the whole world through successions of showers of his beauty like the beauty of millions of Gods of Love.

A form of exhaustion herself inviting and bringing sleep with her, quickly resolved the quarrel between those two made opponents by recognizing the enormity of each other's expertise in the combat of love.

Rising from bed with startled eyes, the women saw that the pleasant, secret sleep of the two monarchs, enjoying a few more moments of pleasure, was unbroken and sat silently on their beds.

Those women questioned each other's late awakening, out of a desire to measure each other's sense of humour, with words punctuated by yawns, each one's dazed and rolling eyes licking at her own breasts like lines of bees.

Then one of them, whose mind was given to the duties (appropriate to the end of the night) of preparing betel nut and

garlands, being moved by *rasa*, having been graced by the fragrance arising from the bodies of the youthful couple bound together by Eros addressed the others:

'O ladies, with your lotus faces pressed to the lattices, cast your eyes into the interior of the cottage and see how sleep embraces and pleases the two lovers, renowned in the dance of intense love.'

Has the God of Love himself caused their clothes to be cast far away as redundant because the two themselves, deeply embracing one another, have clothed each other's bodies in yellow and blue?

The lovers, whose effulgences were like arcs of *champaka* and blue lotus, awoke simultaneously and experienced the pain born of separation due to the stretching of their bodies and as much joy from the deep embrace of their chests.

After opening the door slightly, slowly, and soundlessly, the serving girls, lovely in the careful placement of their feet, became

certain that the lovers were awake and entered the room free of doubt.

The Dear One (Radha), though her desire to get up quickly was increased by the soft, sweet sounds of the girls, trembled intensely because she was not able to force open the arms of her lover.

Softly ringing bangles and ankle bells, the bright complexions of two bodies quickly flying upwards, faces lit up by the glittering of rising necklaces and earrings surrounded by the ends of circles of disordered hair... .

...the loveliness of lotus hands placed here and there out of the confusion of searching for lost clothes; it is as if the beauty of all the three worlds were gathered together in the rising from bed of those two lovers.

Again, because of the contact of their two intensely swaying faces, their loveliness enhanced by the surrounding vine of motionless arms, (they thought), 'Let us for a moment enjoy a little sleep,' and thus they spread out their limbs on the disorderly bed of flowers.

Was it their bed, pained by the agitation of separation, or was it somehow Sleep, having obtained a little taste of their embrace, that was alas unable to give them up at dawn? Nevertheless, the birds singing their songs, succeeded in separating them from those two (bed and Sleep).

✿ *Above:* Radha's handmaiden prepares her for an amorous encouter with her divine lover, Krishna.

❊ 'The joyous festivity of the *rasa*-dance, embellished by the circle of *gopis*, was fully set in motion by Krishna. Then the booming of the kettledrums began, and flowers rained down, as the Gandharva husbands, accompanied by their wives, sang in praise of the untainted Fame of Krishna.'

Radha-Rasa-Sudha-nidhi

A long poem in 284 sanskrit verses, the *Ascharya Rasa Prabandha* is written by Prabodhananda Sarasvati, another of Vrindavana's celebrated Goswamis. This work known as the *Radha-rasa-sudha-nidhi* (the nectar moon of Sri Radha's sweetness) describes Radha and her state of mind and emotions. His language is powerful, often violent, to express the power of the union between the worshipper and God, between a man and a woman.

O Radha, when, after You have spent the entire night enjoying pastimes with the best of charming lovers, and after You have bathed and eaten breakfast with Krishna, will You finally fall asleep, the soles of Your feet gently stroked by my hand?

O my heart, please meditate on the two golden waterpot breasts of King Vrsabhanu's daughter, breasts that are a jewellery chest holding a treasure that is everything to a youth who is like a splendid moon shining in Gokula, a youth whose form, more handsome than millions of Kamadevas, is now manifested in Vrindavana forest.

What is this that I meditate on? Is it two lotus flowers growing in the nectar lake of Sri Radha's passionate love? Or is it two moons manifested from Sri Radha's face? Or is it Sri Radha's youthful breasts? Or is it two monsoon clouds of Sri Radha's nectar bliss.

O Sri Radha, when will I sweetly serve You, who with the arrow of Your sidelong glance deeply wound Vraja's prince, making His peacock feather fall from His turban, the flute fall from His hand, and His yellow garments become disarrayed?

Someday, in the forest grove where They have now met, with great determination I will grasp inexperienced, shy, frightened Sri Radha's lotus hands and lead Her to the bed of the king of lovers, a bed carefully made of soft flower petals.

O Sri Radha, all glory to Your youthfulness, which is filled with many nectar virtues, which carefully sustains Your graceful hips and Your beautiful youthful breasts, graceful like two flower buds, and which has stolen the mind of a person who charms all the worlds.

Sri Radha, O Goddess with glistening curly black hair, glistening *bimba*-fruit lips, a moonlike face, playful *khanjana* bird eyes, a splendid pearl in the tip of Your nose, broad hips, slender waist, splendid breasts, a host of wonderful glories, and vine-arms decorated with graceful armlets, please appear before me.

When will fortunate I see Sri Radha tremble, the hairs on Her charming body erect with joy, as Sri Krishna paints graceful and colourful pictures on her breasts?

She is flooded with perspiration from bringing so many flowers from so far away. The scratches on Her breasts are from thorns. Her *tilaka* was broken by perspiration. Her lips were bitten by the cold winds. O Radha, speaking these words to Your cruel relatives, I will conceal Your meeting with Your beloved.

In this forest the charming girl enjoyed new amorous pastimes. In this place She who is an

---

❋ '"Yadava Hero, your hand is cooler than sandal balm on my breast
"Paint a leaf design with deer musk here on Love's ritual vessel!" She told the joyful hero, playing to delight her heart!'

ocean of nectar danced with Her beloved. O Sri Radha, when will I tremble in the land of Vrindavana as I remember the nectar waves of Your pastimes in this way?

May Sri Radha, whose bodily hairs now stand erect, who, again and again chanting the nectar syllables 'Syama! Syama!' and with longings of love again and again talking of Krishna, now angrily yearns that this day of suffering may somehow pass, protect us.

When will Sri Radha, who passes Her days sometimes singing of Her beloved's skill in amorous pastimes, and sometimes meditating on how in the future She will enjoy with Her beloved, perhaps pretending sweetly to beg Him, 'Enough! Stop! O please stop!' delight us all.

Glory to the fair nectar moon that bears the name '*Radha-rasa-sudha-nidhi*' and which, rising in the sky of the heart, cools the burning fever born from the impersonal sun...

Two youths who eclipse the blue lotus waves of splendour are now reflected on Your breasts. How did they become so charming and enchanting? Please accept them as Your friends and tightly embrace them. May Sri Radha's smile, which appears when Krishna sees His own reflection and speaks these bewildered words, protect us all.

O Radha, when will I see your braids, which are decorated with strings of jewels and flowers, which are gloriously dark like the splendour of sapphires, and which are like a great throne where the king of nectar sits?

O Radha, when will I see Your braids, which with His own hand Krishna has decorated with flowers, jewels, strings of fragrant jasmines, and, at their end, a glistening cluster of rubies?

All glory to the golden cloth that covers your parted hair, a cloth that with its colourful grace fills the heart with wonder, a cloth glistening with pearls and jewels, a cloth filled with all the wonder and sweetness that belongs to the god of love.

O Radha, all glory to the *sindura*-anointed part in Your hair, which seems to say to us, "Because of me the nectar stream of Radha's glistening curly hair is divided into two parts, just like charming, dark, crooked, two-faced Krishna."

What is the nature of Sri Radha's name? It is the sweet nectar of transcendental bliss. What in this book seem to be words describing Sri Radha's feet are actually the splendour of playful Sri Radha's toenails in the graceful and splendid groves of Vrindavana.

Facing page: The *vishwaroopa darshana* that Lord Krishna showed to Arjuna on the battlefield of Kurukshetra. Lord Krishna was Arjun's charioteer during the epic war recorded in the Mahabharata.

the kama texts

there is, in human experience, a connection between sexuality and religion which can be found in all religions and in all ages. In the religions of the post-axial age, *i.e.,* from approximately 500 BCE to the present, sexuality was expressed only esoterically. Indeed as seen in the previous chapter, sexuality in religious thought and expression had often been subsumed by the more abstract theme of love for a higher being. However, though sexuality was often hidden, couched in metaphor and abstraction as well as concealed behind the veils of orthodoxy, it remained a vibrant ingredient in the lives of human beings, a fact borne out by the extensive mythology that surrounds the God of Love.

Eros for the Greeks was originally a very positive figure. For Hesiod, the oldest of the extant Greek poets, he was 'the fairest of the deathless gods'. Similarly, for the Romans, Cupid and Aphrodite signified sexual love as well as beauty. And in India there was Kamadeva about whom much has been written and sung as he personified human desire. This concept that desire is the genesis of the world and is the first seed of all creation makes its appearance very early in Indian scriptural texts where Kama is seen as

being pure cosmic desire. In a beautiful description, this God of Love is portrayed as being the first movement in the primeval chaos, the Prime Mover, the first cause for creation, the God of Gods! Indeed desire is seen as the seed of thought itself and is called *Kamapitamaha*, the Grandfather of Love

In later ages and subsequent mythologies this anthropomorphic form of desire assumes a more sensuous and frolicsome role and becomes synonymous with the erotic sentiment. This then was *kama*, not the god, but desire at its sensual best. Thus in sacred hymns, religious literature, dramaturgy, epic poems, dance, painting, sculpture or music, whatever the form human beings used to express themselves creatively and aesthetically, an element of the erotic crept in almost in deference to a force that was beyond their comprehension and description. This pursuit to know more and the capacity to look in awe and wonder at the mysteries of the world, transformed themselves into aesthetic sensibilities. This does not mean that ancient societies were obsessed with sex. Rather on the contrary. The primary goal of Hindu religious scripture was to encourage and ensure that all human beings, their sexual orientation notwithstanding, would pursue a spiritual life. The emphasis on society was one of balance, where ordinary men and women are exhorted not to eschew desire and its

❋ *Facing page:* Sexuality has always been and remains a vital ingredient in the lives of human beings.

✻ ' When her husband's talk Turned amorous She smiled suggestively At her companions Upon which On one pretext or the other They cheerfully departed.'

attendant emotions, but whole-heartedly embrace passion yet balance it well with the other aspects of living such as *dharma* or righteousness, *artha* or financial well-being. They believed that practising these three aspects of the *purusharthas* added up to the right way of living. Acquiring the right means of seeking a livelihood as well as a balanced sexual life made it possible to lead a meaningful and joyous life. The stress was on stability and

explored not merely the physicality of intercourse but examined its pleasures and pitfalls—impotency, unequal expectations, virility and aphrodisiacs, courtesans, etiquette and manners, thus covering every conceivable aspect of society.

Vedic literature of ancient India has much to contribute towards our understanding of this important issue and that the line between achieving sexual satisfaction and *ananda* or

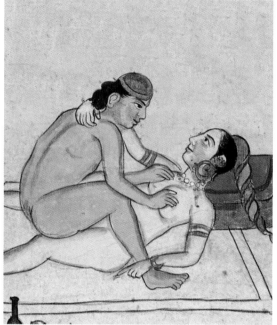

integration; neglecting one of these areas would lead to diminished strength in relationships as well as an imbalance in men.

As part of this search for a balanced existence, the ancients studied sex, practised and dissected it, classified its many methods, shared their knowledge about techniques and passed on what they had learnt. They

bliss is indeed very fine. Seminal works like Panini's *Ashtadhyyayi*, Bharata's *Natyashastra*, Kautilya's *Arthashastra* and of course Vatsyayana's *Kama Sutra* hold a great deal of relevance for modern society as they practically cover all facets of life ranging from right conduct, the value of education, the importance of learning fine arts, issues of

❈ *Above:* 'Stirring the root of her thighs, which her own hands are gripping and holding widely apart, your fluted tongue drinks at her sacred spring: this is known as *Kshobhaka* (Stirring).'

governance and state administration, and sexuality as well. Be it the *Kama Shastras*, the Tantric texts, the Bhakti songs of Radha and Krishna, meditation techniques or even Panini's yoga, all these works strive to explore the hidden dimensions of the unity of the body and the mind, which modern science is only now beginning to understand. The ancients explored and understood the various aspects of human life, its main tenets and

seeking becomes a personal adventure which is not merely to acquire intellectual and ego-satisfying trivia but a quest for the wisdom to influence and shape events.

All these works, therefore point towards a radically different view about sexuality: to view sex as a lawful, if limited expression of bliss, but more importantly, as a means of getting in touch with a higher consciousness. It has often been hypothesized that these

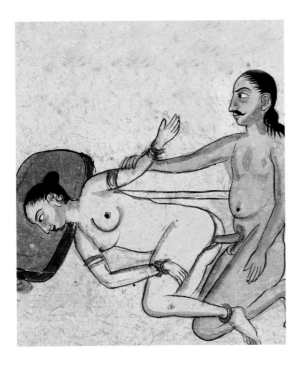 

attractions, and used the energies of the mind, body and intellect to rise about the mundane. None of these works are religious but their philosophy is deeply rooted in the traditional, religious and spiritual beliefs of India. All these texts emphasize the need for knowledge and that it should be obtained through firsthand experience. Thus the very act of

books of Kama teachings came into existence because of frustrations in married life in a patriarchal society where marriages were arranged for convenience and where love was uncommon. In truth, ancient and medieval India was a vibrant society that not just lived but celebrated life it in all its aspects, without hypocrisy or guilt.

✷ *Above:* 'You lift her ankles high; she draws up and extends her legs as though she were crawling through the air: this is *Hastika* (the Elephant).'

❊ 'In the pleasure room, decorated with flowers, and fragrant with perfumes, attended by his friends and servants, the *nayak* should receive the woman, who will come bathed and dressed, and will invite her to partake of refreshment and to drink freely.'

the kama sutra

Vatsyayana urges the study of the text in order to achieve the fullness of pleasure that humans solely can obtain in sexual union, which he believes can result from following the procedure he describes. Vatsyayana begins by saying that, although Vatsyayana was a man writing for men, a large part of the text directly addresses women as it recognizes them too as full participants in sex. It frequently warns and advises women on all the facets of their relationships with men, be that about attracting men, fobbing them off pleasantly, entertaining them, or changing them! The sage wisely exhorts men to learn ejaculatory control to last long enough to bring women to orgasm: 'Women love the man whose sexual energy lasts a long time, but they resent a man whose energy ends quickly because he stops before they reach a climax.'

'A woman being of a tender nature wants tender beginnings,' and lays a great deal of emphasis on the need for both partners to be attentive and stresses the importance of foreplay, embracing, kissing, and other types of touching calculated to heighten sexual arousal. The groundwork, he believes, is as important as the act itself: 'In the pleasure room, decorated with flowers, and fragrant with perfumes, attended by his friends and servants, the *nayak* should receive the woman, who will come bathed and dressed, and will invite her to partake of refreshment and to drink freely. He should then seat her on his left side, and holding her hair, and touching the end knot of her garment, should gently embrace her with his right arm. They should then carry on an amusing conversation on various subjects, and may also talk suggestively of things which would be considered as coarse, or not to be mentioned generally in society. They may then sing, either with or without gesticulations, and play on musical instruments, talk about the arts, and persuade each other to drink. At last when the woman is overcome with love and desire, the citizen should dismiss the people that may be with him. Then presenting her with flowers, perfumes and betel they should proceed… .

Congress is of the following kinds:

* Loving congress

* Congress of subsequent love

* Congress of artificial love

* Congress of transferred love

* Congress like that of eunuchs

* Deceitful congress

* Congress of spontaneous love

* *Facing page:* Sexual love is an expression of divine love binding two souls to each other in a union that provides a foretaste of the ultimate union with the Supreme Being where all else fades into oblivion and ceases to matter altogether.

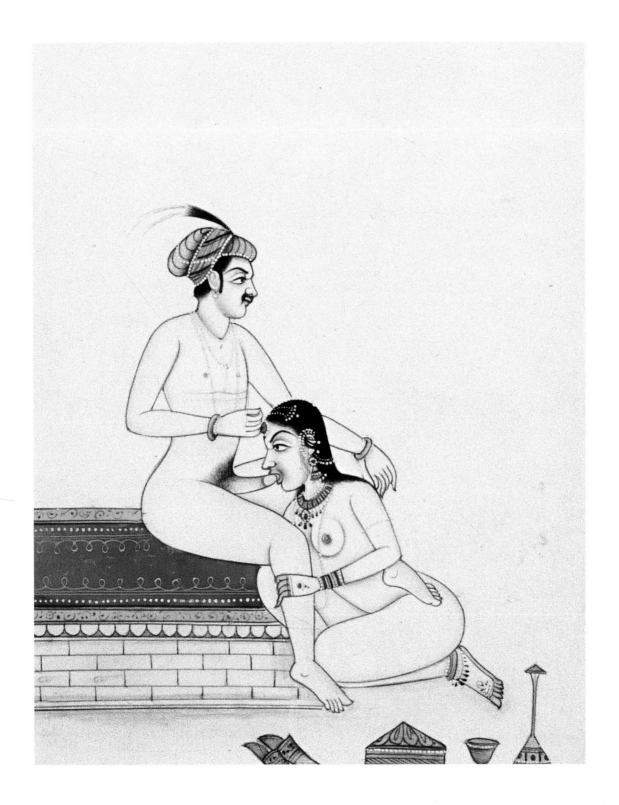

❋ 'Fired by passion, she takes you deep into her mouth, pulling and sucking as vigorously as though stripping clean a mango: this is the *Amrachushita* (Sucking a Mango).'

❋ If a man and a woman learn how to swing to each other's
rhythm, their love will never become stale.

The best known of the Kama literature is of course, Vatsyayana's *Kama Sutra*, which was compiled around the third century CE. It is a comprehensive guide on etiquette, social behaviour, the niceties of interpersonal intimacy, and the nuances of the unwritten yet subtle code of affection underlining man-woman relationships. Vatsyayana clearly states that much of the condemnation of sexual practices is due to abnormal expressions and perversions rather than due to a healthy concern for it. The *Kama Sutra* is nothing less than a social treatise with its very modern focus on private behaviour and a detailed even painstaking emphasis on conventions, artifices, and graces that attend to social and sexual intercourse.

Besides the now famous chapters of sexual positions, the role of the courtesan, seduction of other women, the emphasis on kissing, embracing, biting, leaving nail marks, among other things, the book also advocates the use of sex toys, aphrodisiacs and remedies for impotency and low sexual drive. It describes in detail how a man can best satisfy two women at the same time (fondle one while having intercourse with the other), and how two or more men should comport themselves when sexually sharing one woman (take turns having intercourse, and while one is inside her, the others should fondle her).

The *Kama Sutra* may be the world's most famous book on sex, but it was by no means the first. Nor was it the last. Starting from the *Rg Veda*, written some 4000 years ago which records the romance between a mortal king called Pururavasa and a celestial nymph known as Urvashi, as well as an incestuous dialogue between the Lord of Death, Yama, and his twin sister Yami, to the epic Mahabharata, where the impotent King Pandu exhorts his wife Kunti to seek other men to beget children and thus keep alive his lineage, to the extremely sensuous works of poets like Kalidasa and Amaru, the first millennium was a time of quest, discovery and self-expression, and of erotic pleasure, among other things.

These concepts of sexuality underwent change as the world entered the second millennium. Paradoxically even as the Middle Ages saw the emergence of stricter social systems as well as a new morality that maintained that logic and free-thinking were acts against the *Dharma Shastras*, the preoccupation with things sexual increased multifold. Even as social norms became more rigid, India's artistic sensibilities found erotic expression in ink, paint and stone. Medieval India saw sensuousness creep into every aesthetic expression. Thus a thousand years after the *Kama Sutra*, the Chandella kings (950-1050 AD) built one of the finest groups of temples in India at their capital Khajuraho. In stark contrast to synagogues, churches or mosques worldwide, the Indian temple from the 8th century onwards incorporated the most intimate and personal of human interactions, in full public view breaking down the shackles of hypocritical prudery. All forms of sexual depiction, ranging from the heterosexual, homosexual as well as auto-erotic attitudes of men and women, including gods and goddesses, members of the aristocracy, ascetics to group sexuality and

❋ *Facing page:* 'She draws her limbs together, clasping her knees tightly to her breasts, her *yoni*, like an opening bud, offered up for pleasure: this is the *Mukula* (the Bud).'

❋ The *Kama Sutra* is a social treatise which focuses on private behaviour and painstakingly lays emphasis on conventions, artifices, and graces that attend to social and sexual intercourse.

❉ 'She bends well forward and grips the bedstead, her buttocks raised high; cup your hands to serpents' hoods and squeeze her jar-shaped breasts together: this is *Dhenuka* (the Milch Cow).'

bestiality were displayed almost defiantly on the exteriors as well as in the interiors of the temples. Regionalism, the development of local dialects and languages, changing social conventions too all came together to strongly influence cultural life. By the 10th century, sensuality and sexual interaction had already left their indelible marks not just in the temples of Khajuraho but in Konarak, Bhubaneshwar, in the Kakathiya temples of

So between the 10th and 18th centuries, several texts similar to the *Kama Sutra* were written, most of them by noblemen and kings, who refined the art of courtship and love-making while adding their own experiences and interpretations. There were reasons why the Middle Ages saw an explosion of erotic texts after a hiatus of almost 800 years. For one, the curiosity and interest in sexuality continued unabated.

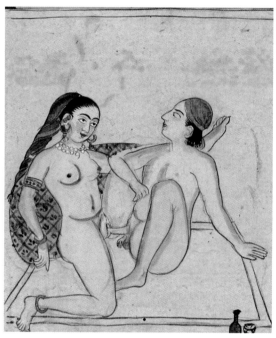

Palampet and in the numerous lesser-known temples of the Rajasthan and Chhattisgarh region. Besides the temple carvings, the *nayak-nayika* paintings as well as erotic Bhakti poetry outpourings, all reinforced the idea that religion did not eschew sexuality, but rather accepted it in a wise, mature and egalitarian manner, so as to ensure the emotional health and well-being of society.

Having already established a tradition of being a sensuous society, the attempt was to keep alive the knowledge of knowing what to do, as well as the proper manner and techniques to do it. These texts, like the *Kama Sutra*, were based on the principle of physical gratification and that pleasure was the ultimate goal. Much of the later Kama literature such as the *Rati-rahasya* of Kokkoka,

✤ *Above:* The *Kama Shastra* texts are based on the principle of physical gratification and seeking fulfilment is the ultimate goal of human existence.

the *Nagarasarvasvam* of Padmasri, and the *Jayamangala* commentary of Yasodhara, imitate the *Kama Sutra*. A notable feature of several of these classic texts on erotica is their near-obsession with classification. Taking their cue from the *Kama Sutra*, these latter-day manuals, too became particularly adept at cataloguing not just positions and postures but types of lovers, categories of men and women depending on their personality and

observation and a great deal of research and study.

The earliest of these latter-day texts is surprisingly a Buddhist work called the *Nagarasarvasvam* or *A Guide for a Townsman*. Written by a monk called Bhikshu Padmasri, it is an extant 10th-century work. Buddhist erotic texts are rare although even the Buddha is known to have used metaphors to narrate moral tales, as is illustrated in the

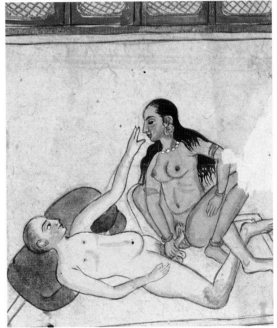

temperament, the size of the phallus and the vagina, and more. The protagonists in the erotic play were unrelentingly further classified in accordance with their mood and emotions, their meeting places and the disposition of their personality. However, it is equally true that for all their excess, the classifications were based on very astute

Jataka tales. But this is a very modern book that focuses on imparting valuable information on how to be a successful dandy or *nayak*. Essentially a gentleman's how-to-do-it guide, it deals with, besides other things, the nuances of etiquette, seduction, and the need to interpret body language and gestures.

✤ *Above:* Erotic Bhakti poetry reinforced the idea that religion did not eschew sexuality, rather it accepted it in a wise, mature, and egalitarian manner, so as to ensure the emotional health and well-being of society.

✤ *Following pages 120-121:* There is no particular time or place for love as long as lovers are willing to unite with each other to experience bliss.

Rati-Rahasya

The 11th-century *Rati-rahasya*, which translates as *Secrets of Love*, was written by a poet who has come to be known as Kokkoka. The work contains nearly 800 verses, and is divided into ten chapters, which are called *Pachivedas*. The book is different from the *Kama Sutra* as it contains the four classifications of women known as the *Padmini* (woman resembling a lotus), *Chitrini* (deer-like woman), *Shankini* (woman who resembles a conch shell) and *Hastini* (Elephant woman), as also the enumeration of the days and hours on which women of different classes become subject to love, as well as a very detailed chapter on 'love cries':

Love Blows and Love Cries

Experience tells us that striking the back of the hand between the breasts evokes the moaning sound. The back should be struck with the knuckles and with the hand bent into the shape if a cobra's hood, while blows on the sides and genitals are given with the flat of the hand. The shears and other types of striking, which are used in the south, are disapproved by the masters.

With the girl sitting on his knee, the lover should strike her on the back with one fist. She will pretend to be angry and retaliate, screaming, gasping and becoming drunken with love. Towards the end of intercourse, he will strike very gently and continuously over the heart of the girl while she is still penetrated and at each stroke she will give the cry of 'sit'. If she tussles with him, he will strike on her head with the curved hand and in response she will give the sounds of 'kat' and 'phut' and will gasp or moan. Just before orgasm he will strike quickly repeated blows with the flat of the hand on her genital and her sides. If her passion begins to wane, the Lady-of-the Buttocks will utter cries like those of the quail or *hamsa*. After her climax, she may again scream or gasp repeatedly. At other times, too, a woman will utter love cries that make her infinitely desirable without being either in pain or weary of intercourse.

Passion and roughness in copulation combined with tenderness usually make only the man attractive but according to local and other customs a short exchange of roles from passion can be delightful.

Just as a spirited horse takes no heed of obstacles at full gallop, so too, lovers while making love take no heed for blows or hard knocks. But it is the duty of the man to consider the tastes of women and to be tough or gentle entirely in accordance to his beloved's wishes.

❋ *Facing page:* The primary duty of a loyal wife is to have intercourse with her husband; therefore she should energetically and enthusiastically be prepared to make love always.

✳ 'As soon as she commences to enjoy pleasure, the eyes are half closed and watery, the body waxes cold, her breath becomes hard and jerky, is expired in sobs or sighs... '

✳ 'Her lower limbs are limply stretched out after a period of rigidity; a rising and outflow of love and affection appear, with kisses and sportive gestures and finally she seems like she is about to swoon.'

the ananga ranga

After the *Kama Sutra* and the *Koka Shastra*, the *Ananga Ranga* of Kalyanamalla is the most influential of Indian erotic texts. Written probably in the 15th century, the book is dedicated to one Lad Khan, the son of Ahmad Khan, of the House of the Lodis and reads: 'by the great Princely Sage and Arch poet Kalyanamalla, versed in all the arts'. The work too has candid and forthright descriptions. For instance, the very first chapter gives the characteristics of the four main types of women and the appropriate days to enjoy them… . The second narrates the erogenous zones of women, the third deals with the three types of men and women based on the length and depth of their sex organs and the nine types of unions.

of different kinds of men and women

men

There are three kinds of men, namely the *Shasha* or the Hare man, the *Vrishaba* or Bull man and the *Ashwa* or Horse man. They may be described by explanation of their nature and by enumeration of their accidents.

The *Shasha* is known by a *lingam*, which in erection does not exceed six fingers breadth, or about three inches. His figure is short and spare but well proportioned in shape and make. He has small hands, knees, feet, loins and thighs, the latter being darker than the rest of his skin. His features are clear and well proportioned; his face is round, his teeth are short and fine, his hair is silky and his eyes are large and well. He is of quiet disposition, he does good for virtues sake, he is humble in demeanor, his appetite for food is small and he is moderate in carnal desires. Finally there is nothing offensive in his *kama-salila* or semen.

The *Vrishaba* is known by a *lingam* of nine fingers in length or four inches and a half. His body is robust and tough like that of a tortoise, his chest is fleshy, and his belly is hard. His forehead is high; his eyes large and long with pink corners and the palms of his hand are red. His disposition is cruel and violent and his *kama-salila* is ever ready.

The *Ashwa* is known by a *lingam* of 12 fingers or about six inches long. He is tall and well framed but not fleshy and his delight is in big and robust women. Never in those of a delicate form. His body is hard as iron, his chest is broad, full and muscular, his body below the hips is long and the same is the case with his mouth and teeth, his neck and ears, while his hands are remarkably so. His knees are somewhat crooked and this distortion may also be observed in the nails of his toes. He is reckless in spirit, passionate and covetous, gluttonous, volatile, lazy and full of sleep. He cares little for venereal rites except when the spasm approaches. His *kama-salila* is copious, salty and goat-like.

❊ *Facing page:* 'A woman who thus has intercourse with her husband in the month of Phagun attains wealth, male children, grandchildren, grain and prosperity. She is considered to be blessed.'

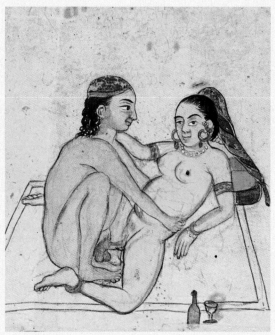

women

As men are divided into three classes by the length of the *lingam*, so the four orders of women—*Padmini, Chitrini, Shankini* and *Hastini* may be sub-divided into three kinds according to the depth and extent of their *yoni*. These are the *Mrigi* also called *Harini*, the Deer woman; the *Vadava* or *Ashvini*, the Mare woman and the *Karini*, or Elephant woman.

The *Mrigini* has a *yoni* six fingers deep. Her body is delicate with a girlish aspect, soft and tender. Her head is small; her bosom stands up well, her stomach is thin and drawn in, her thighs and *mons veneris* are fleshy and her build below the hips is solid. Her hair is thick and curly, her eyes are black as the dark lotus flower; her nostrils are fine; her cheeks and ears are large, her hands, feet and lower lip are ruddy and her fingers are straight. Her voice is that of the Kokila bird and her gait the rolling of the elephant. She eats

moderately but is much addicted to the pleasures of love. She is affectionate but jealous and she is active in mind when not subdued by her passions. Her *kama-salila* has the pleasant perfume of the lotus flower.

The *Vadava* or *Ashwini* numbers nine inches depth. Her body is delicate, her arms are thick from the shoulders, her breasts and hips broad and fleshy and her umbilical region is high raised but without a protuberant stomach. Her hands and feet are red like flowers and well proportioned. Her head slopes forward and is covered with long straight hair. She has a graceful walk and she loves sleep and good living. Though choleric and versatile, she is affectionate to her husband but does not readily reach orgasm and her *kama-salila* is perfumed like the lotus.

The *Karini* has a *yoni* twelve fingers in depth. Unclean in her person, she has large breasts and her nose, ears and throat are long and thick, her

❈ *Above:* Passion and roughness in copulation combined with tenderness can be a delightful experience.

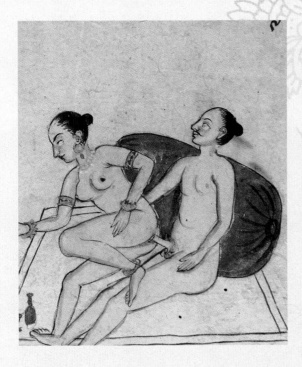 

lips are long and bent, her face is broad, her hair thick and blackish. Her eyes are fierce and yellow tinged, her feet, hands and arms are short and fat, her teeth are large and sharp as a dog's. She is noisy when eating, her voice is hard, she is gluttonous and her joints crack with movement. Of a wicked and utterly shameless disposition, she never hesitates to commit sin. Excited and disquieted by carnal desires, she is not easily satisfied and requires congress unusually protracted. Her *kama-salila* is abundant and it suggests the juice that flows from the elephant's temples... .

Before proceeding to the various acts of congress the symptoms of the orgasm in women must be laid down. As soon as she commences to enjoy pleasure, the eyes are half closed and watery, the body waxes cold, her breath becomes hard and jerky, is expired in sobs or sighs; the lower limbs are limply stretched out after a period of rigidity; a rising and outflow of love and affection appear, with kisses and sportive gestures and finally she seems like she is about to swoon. At such a time, a distaste for further embraces becomes manifest, then the wise one knows that the paroxysm having taken place, the woman has enjoyed plenary satisfaction; they refrain from further congress.

❋ *Above:* Excited and disquietened by carnal desire she is not easily satisfied and requires congress that is unusually protracted.

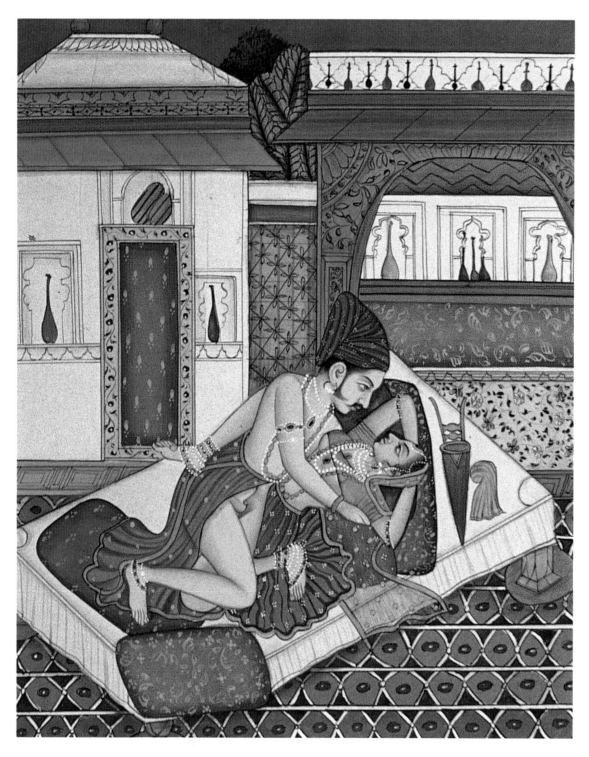

✻ 'A beauteous woman completely dispels despair in men. Kissing her brings on the fever of love, embracing her brings freshness and coolness like the moon and sandalwood paste, and to have *maithuna* with her is like being in heaven—the abode of the gods.'

✤ 'Which is why the man should give himself to her and kiss her lotus-like lips. Such a man becomes ecstatic and is blessed. The one who has intercourse, kissing her on the lips and entering her gets reborn on earth with renewed strength and vigour.'

Others texts such as the *Smaradipika, Ratiratnapradipika,* Kavishekara's *Panchasayaka* and *Manmatha Sutram* also emerged from various parts of the country, never actually veering away from the general grid laid down by Vatsyayana. A very elegant work called the *Ratimanjari* for example classifies women according to their age:

give and take of love, the old woman to hard knocks.

The young girl gives a man pleasure and the breathe of life (*prana*), the young woman draws out the breathe of life, the *praudha* brings old age, the old woman brings death....

The penis of a man is described by experts as being of two kinds, the club

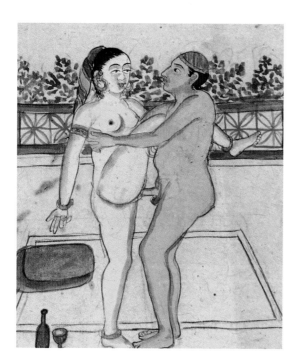

Until sixteen years a young girl is a *bala,* until thirty she is a young woman (*taruni*) until fifty-five an experienced woman (*praudha*) and an old woman (*vrddha*) thereafter.

The young girl is a lover of flowers and sweet things; the young woman is given to love play, the *praudha* to the

of the whistle, the first is stout and the second is long and thin... .

A man who is fond of women, a good singer, cheerful, having a penis six fingerbreadths long and clever such is a hare (*sasaka*).

One who is a paragon, virtuous, truthful and courteous, having an

❧ *Above:* The essence of the world that brings happiness to all people is sex. Undermining sexual happiness is akin to turning one's back upon the pathway to bliss.

132

eight-finger penis and handsome such is a gazelle (*mrga*).

One who is serviceable, uxorious, phlegmatic, with a ten-finger member and prudent such is a bullock (*vrsa*).

One who is tough, with a body of solid wood, insolent, of deceitful habits, fearless, with a twelve-finger penis, and no money such is a stallion (*asva*).

is said to have spent 86,000 years practising the art of seduction and thus imminently qualified to have written this treatise on the science of sexual love. This ancient text by Pururava has a latter-day, 15th-century commentary and presents a new genre in writing, in that the verses are succinct, almost terse in their brevity without any attempt at the usual elaborate literary style

And then there is an early 14th-century work—*Pururavasamanasijasutram*—resulting from a romantic interlude between the emperor Pururava and the best-known of celestial nymphs, Urvashi. This is one of the oldest known romances ever to be recorded, appearing first in the *Rg Veda* (10.95) *c.*1500 BC. Pururava, a statesman and wise emperor

for which Sanskrit poetry was renowned. They indeed read like factual statements, devoid of any sensual element. Also known as the *Manmatha Sutram* after Manmatha, the God of Love, it describes the different kinds of *ananda* or bliss. It says that the immediate goal of all sentient beings is to seek *sukha,* or happiness, the final beatitude being known

❀ *Above:* Thus to attain maximum happiness and bliss everyone should experience the bliss of sex.

❀ *Following pages 134-135:* Women being sensitive by nature need to be courted artfully in order to win their affection.

as *mahasukha* or *ananda* literally, 'great happiness' best described as bliss.

The *Pururavasamanasijasutram* attempts to explain the aim and techniques to achieve sexual gratification and the resultant bliss. The belief therefore is that an in-depth knowledge of the *Kama Shastras* is mandatory if we want to evolve from animalism to humanism and thence to divinity.

The bliss that can be attained from sexual love has been divided into four parts and involves four procedures:

Pressing both the breasts of the woman against one's chest is known as *Ratiananda*.

Drinking the nectar of her genitals is the cause of the highest bliss.

The complete insertion of the penis deep into the temple of love is the physical cause and means of attaining *Brahmanand*.

The half insertion of the penis is the cause of the bliss of *Lekharsabha*.

Ananda or bliss is a word that is also used to describe the *Parabrahman* or the Supreme Being and this blissful state, it was thought, could be achieved through both mystical and aesthetic experiences. Indian philosophy from the earliest times has always believed that fulfilment and happiness in life is a result of the sacred fusion of the body, mind and soul. It is believed that an orgasm most closely simulates the absolute bliss that human beings consciously or unconsciously strive for, and this pleasure, though ephemeral, creates a momentary state of balance and oneness with a higher being. Therefore, various stages of finding *ananda* or bliss through intercourse are named after the abode of the gods and are variously known as *Ratianand, Brahmanand, Indranand,* to name just a few. The *lokas* or worlds refer to the manifold experiences that one goes through during a lifetime. Different desires find fulfilment in various stages of experiences, from *Lokanand* or the pleasures of the world to the happiness experienced in *Brahmalok* that is said to provide the highest of sensuous enjoyments.

The list of seminal works on erotic literature in India is endless. The belief that the study of the *Shastras* would unravel the nature of one's desires and help in exploring and understanding the relationship between passion, desire, happiness and satisfaction in the clear light of firsthand knowledge, was the basis on which these books were written. All *Kama Shastra* books including Vatsayana's *Kama Sutra* believed that right knowledge is all about seeking and finding a balance between all human urges: physical, emotional, intellectual, social, sexual, spiritual. These texts thus strive to heighten the level of psychosomatic energies and intensify awareness, until finally, there is a breakthrough into the transcendental dimension of bliss.

✽ *Facing page:* Fulfilment and happiness in life result from the sacred fusion of the body, mind and soul, represented by an orgasm as it most closely simulates the absolute bliss that human beings consciously or unconsciously strive for.

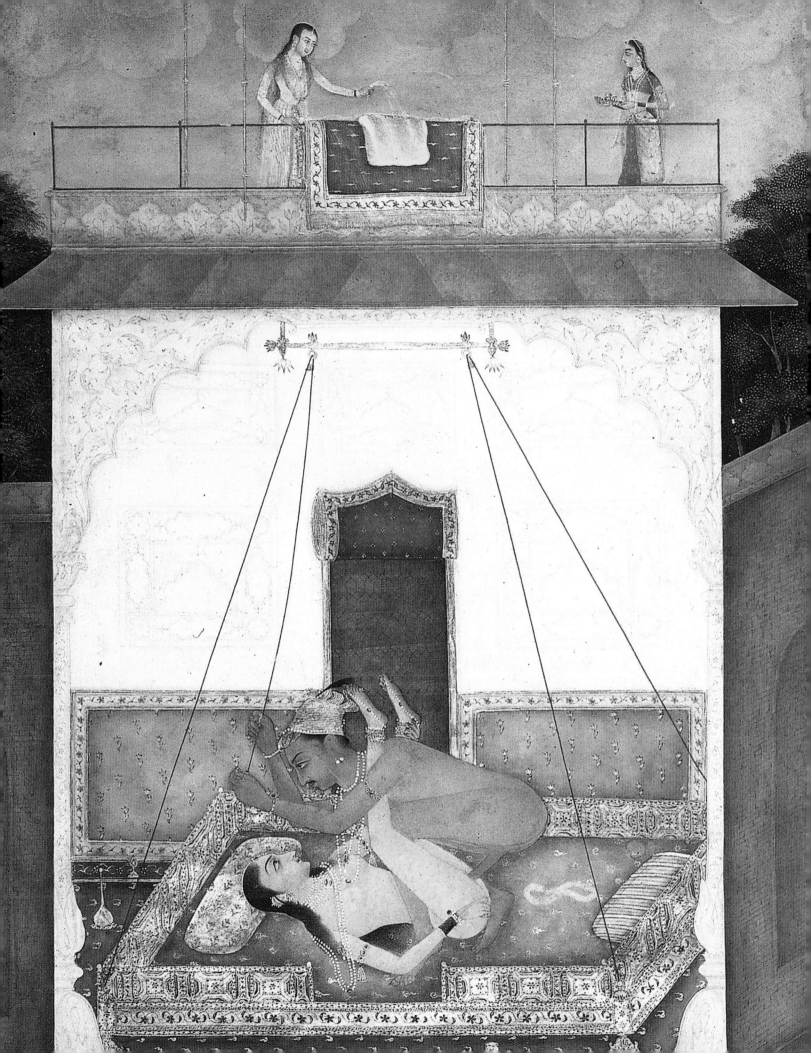

tantra

The Tantric tradition in India is said to pre-date the coming of the Aryans and constitutes the basic teachings of both Puranic Hindu culture as well as folk religions especially those based on fertility cults. This tradition is not restricted to India, Nepal and Tibet, and existed in the Far East, Polynesia, and indigenous cultures all over the world. Apparently even the North American Cherokees practised a form of Tantra called *Quadoshka*, which used the body as a vehicle to achieve cosmic realization and union with divinity. The word 'tantra' has many definitions. Some claim it comes from Sanskrit and means to weave or hold together; others say that it is an amalgam of two Sanskrit words 'tanoti' and 'trayati': tanoti means to expand one's awareness while *trayati* means to liberate consciousness. In yet another sense, *tantra* also means the scripture by which the light of knowledge is spread. Whichever way the word is interpreted, Tantra is a means to expand as well as liberate consciousness, making it the very fabric of existence.

Yet, of all the forms of *Hindu Shastra*, Tantra is the least known and most misunderstood, mainly due to the esoteric nature of its subject matter, and the fact that the key to much of its terminology and method rests with the initiate. Tantra is often thought of to be nothing more than black magic and its practitioners, black magicians. Despite this Tantra caught the imagination of a nation as it crossed the strict moral codes and taboos, all boundaries and confines and combined the ancient fertility tradition in nature with the contemplative and sacred in Indian tradition. It interprets physical love as an integrated biological and spiritual manifestation of genesis. Built on the belief that there is a connection between the cosmos and human beings that has become polarized, its ultimate goal is to bridge this apparent duality and seek *ananda* or bliss. Men and women represent this duality but attempt to overcome their sense of separateness during sexual union thereby attempting to engage all conscious aspects of reality into one integrated whole. This metaphorical representation was not restricted to Tantra alone, rather the same concepts were in the conjugated metamorphosis of Ishtar-Tamuz in Babylon, of Prajna-Vajra in Buddhism, of Sophia-Christos in Christianity, Isis-Osiris in Egypt and even in the esoteric teachings of the Kabala. Tantrics believe that the greatest source of energy in the universe is sexual, that orgasm is a cosmic and divine experience. Therefore, they place great value on sacred sexuality or ritualized intercourse. They further believe that intercourse heightens these energies and should be utilized for spiritual growth and healing.

Despite this, Tantra is not about sex for it uses the erotic experience to transcend sexuality. Unlike the Vedic percepts of 'Nothingness' or *Sat-Chit-Ananda* (Consciousness-Being-Bliss), Tantrics relied on the human body as a more tangible form of worship, for the belief was that human beings needed practical methods for realizing the divine rather than resorting to mere metaphysical concepts. This led to a very practical approach to sexuality which lay in the recognition that instead of abusing the body and living in denial and renunciation, a better path was to acknowledge it. So rather than attempting to 'master the flesh' by punishing it or ignoring it, Tantrics mastered it by using it as a vehicle to spirituality. They believed that the body is a temple to the deity within. Hence, the most important vehicle for attaining *ananda* or bliss is the human being, as Tantra visualizes the body as being a microcosmic representation of the universe through which cosmic powers are revealed. According to Tantric principles, all that exists in the universe must also exist in the individual body and one way of understanding the mysteries of the universe is to search for the truth within.

According to the *Ratnasara,* a Tantra text, 'He who realizes the truth of the body can then come to know the truth of the universe.' Thus Tantrics saw sexuality as an ally, rather than a hindrance to enlightenment.

This practical approach to seeking the divine also led to the constitution of an *ishta devta* or a personal deity/god, who usually took the forms of Shiva and Shakti who in turn represent the very essence of creation. Besides this there are two kinds of yoga in Tantric practices. In Mantra yoga, meditation is focused on mystical mantras or hymns and geometric drawings known as *mandalas* or *yantras*. Laya yoga or Kundalini yoga focuses on an elaborate mystical physiology. *Laya* means 'dissolution,' and refers to the dissolution of the macrocosm (the universe) within the microcosm which in this case is the Tantric's own body, and ultimately, to the dissolution of this empirical self into the deity. Kundalini yoga, another name for the same process, means coiled-up and represents the female energy or Shakti existing in a latent form, not only in every human being but in every atom of the universe. During Kundalini yoga, this serpentine power is aroused and proceeds up the series of seven lotus centres also known as *chakras* until it reaches a point just above the head, which symbolizes the masculine Supreme Self (Shiva consciousness). When Shakti and Shiva consciousness meet, a state of awakening and liberation is attained. Instances of common practice are for example *mantra* (sacred chant), *bija mantra* (the seed or root vowel), *yantra* (instrument), *mudra* (symbol), *nyasa* (place). All this turned Tantra into a highly ritualized form of spiritual practice

✤ *Facing page:* Kundalini yoga focuses on an elaborate mystical physiology and refers to the dissolution of the macrocosmic universe into the microcosm which is the Tantric's own body.

❋ 'Lord Shiva wandering in a forest looking for alms came about the wives of sages who were immediately struck with wonder and became attracted to Sambhu. Saying, "There is no doubt that women can give you pleasure by their mere touch," the young women gathered around him.'

❋ *Facing page:* 'Woman is the creator of the universe
The universe is her form
Woman is the foundation of the world
She is the true form of the body
In woman is the form of all things.'

abetted further by the construction and consecration of temples and images, religious and social observances, as well as the practice of practical magic known as Maya yoga.

The best known of all the Tantric rituals is the *panchatattvas* which derives its name from the Sanskrit words '*pancha*' (five) and '*tattva*' (element). The five elements used in this ritual are *madya* (wine), *mamsa* (meat), *matsya* (fish), *mudra* (parched corn) and *maithuna* (sexual union). The symbolism of *madya* was that for all those people who were dominated by their physical instincts the Lord (usually Shiva) instructed them to continue drinking wine, but he showed them how to control the habit and then finally leave it. The same holds true for the concept of eating *mamsa*. For those who ate much meat, Shiva told them to continue but finally control the urge. A more subtle interpretation of *mamsa* is that it refers to the tongue and the practice of controlling one's speech. The third of these rituals involved the *matsya* where the same instructions hold as for the wine and meat.

❋ *Above:* 'There is neither passion nor absence of passion. Seated beside her own, her mind destroyed, Thus I have seen the *yogini*.'

144

Mudra has only a spiritual significance and is meant to maintain contact with those who help make spiritual progress and to avoid the company of those who might harm development. The last of these, *maithuna,* in its crudest form signifies sexual union. And here again for those who were dominated by the sexual instinct, it has been advised that the act of intercourse has to be performed keeping in mind that the idea behind this union is only symbolic of the union of the individual consciousness with the Supreme Consciousness. In this case the spiritual energy of the human being, lying dormant at the base of the spine, is raised until it reaches the highest energy centre causing the spiritual aspirant to experience union with the Supreme Consciousness.

These *panchatattvas* were an intrinsic part of Shakti worship where the union of Shiva and Shakti came to be represented by this idea of *maithuna.* It was said that a man by uniting with his wife according to these rites, experienced the same bliss as of the great union between Shiva and Shakti.

These various aspects of the Tantric system gained expediency between the 6th and 11th centuries probably as an overt consequence of the rigours and excesses of brahmanical morality and orthodoxy. The re-emergence of the ancient mother goddess cults further nurtured this movement that attempted to integrate sexual license and spirituality. The practice of Tantra took root and flourished in Bengal and Assam, Kerala and Kashmir where the worship of the *yoni* or the female organ became an elaborate ritual, and an end in itself. The *yoni* in both Hindu and Buddhist Tantra texts is often likened to the lotus, revered for its beauty, perfection, fragrance and symmetry. Venerated for its obvious properties of fertility and growth, the *yoni*

was seen as the centre of concentrated energy or *tejas* which when stimulated gave birth to all creation. In Tantra too, the taboo of menstrual blood, and seeing it as unclean and unhealthy, breaks down for in the Tantric tradtion, while worshipping the *yoni* the menstrual fluid is regarded as sacred. In most Tantric practices as specified in the texts, a menstruating woman is regarded as special for her energy at this time is said to be different in quality, and the body rhythms in tune with the mysterious processes of nature. In the Chakra-puja of the left-hand Tantrics, menstrual fluid was drunk as part of a ritual along with wine, and a special homage paid to the menstruating *yoni,* touching it with one's lips and anointing it with sandalwood paste. In a number of Tantric texts, the woman as epitomized by Shakti is the dominant lover of a quiescent Shiva, this union being critical for him to be able to assert his divinity and powers. The very first verse of the *Saundarya Lahiri* states: 'If Shiva is united with his Shakti he is able to exert his powers as a Lord; if not, the god has not even the strength to move.' She is the potency that dwells in each of the male gods and the spark that arouses them to action. A related aspect of deviational sex was the emphasis placed by the *sadhaka* or devotee to deriving the benefits of the female energy without loss of his own semen, for it was widely regarded that the ability to control ejaculation and retain the seed within was a guarantor of prolonged virility and potency.

Most Tantric texts make for very erotic reading and are known as *Agamas* which belong to the Shakta cult which glorifies Shakti as the World-Mother. There are seventy-seven such *Agamas*, usually in the form of a dialogue between Shiva and Parvati. The best-known Hindu Tantric

texts are the *Mahanirvana, Kularnava, Kulasara, Prapanchasara, Tantraraja, Rudra Yamala, Brahma Yamala, Vishnu Yamala,* and the *Todala Tantra* which explore and reveal several occult practices, some of which confer powers, while others bestow knowledge and freedom. Of all these texts the *Yoni Tantra,* an 11th-century religious text from Bengal, is of special interest. *Maithuna* or sexual union is an indispensable part of this Tantric ritual as the book is dedicated to *Yoni puja,* or worship of the vulva. Best described as a eulogy of the *yoni* and the *yoni tattva,* the text specifies nine types of women, twelve to sixty years of age, married or single, who can perform these sexual rituals.

According to the Kaula Tantrics, the most sacred spot in India is Kamarupa in Assam where the genitals of the Devi fell after her body was sliced into 51 parts by the discus of Vishnu. Legend has it that a young lady known as Madhavi who lived there was renowned for the beauty of her *yoni* which was venerated by Shiva himself. This Tantric text refers to the ten *Mahavidyas,* the different incarnations of Madhavi or Parvati, each of who are associated with an aspect of the *yoni* worthy of worship.

The Yoni Tantra, contains eight *patalas,* that describe in detail the worship of the *yoni.* Some are mentioned below:

Seated on the peak of Mount Kailasha, the God of Gods, the guru of all creation, was questioned by Durga, 'Lord, sixty-four Tantras have been created. Tell me, Ocean of Compassion, about the chief of these.'

Mahadeva said: 'Listen, dearest Parvati, to this great secret. There are mantras called *pitha, yantra pitha* and *yoni pitha.* Among these, the chief is certainly the *yoni pitha.* A *yoni* worshipper should prepare the Shakti mantra. If a person worships with menstrual flowers, he also has power over fate. The devotee should place a Shakti in a circle. She should be wanton, beautiful, devoid of shame and disgust, charming by nature, supremely alluring and beautiful. He should place her on his left, and should worship her hair-adorned *yoni.* At the edges of the *yoni,* the devotee should place sandal and beautiful blossoms. There, in drawing the goddess, he should do *jiva*

❀ *Above:* 'She should be wanton, beautiful, devoid of shame and disgust, charming by nature, supremely alluring and beautiful. He should place her on his left, and should worship her hair-adorned *yoni.*'

nyasa using mantra, having given her wine and drawing a half-moon using vermilion. After smearing sandal on her forehead, the devotee should caress her breasts. After reciting the mantra 108 times, while in her arms, the devotee should caress the breasts, having previously kissed her on the cheek. The mantra should be recited 108 or 1008 times in the *yoni* circle.

❋

The Devi said: 'God of Gods, which types of *yoni* should be worshipped and what brings good fortune?'

The devotee should have intercourse with all *yonis*. He may have intercourse with any woman between the ages of twelve and sixty. He should worship the *yoni* daily, using the five *tattvas*. By seeing the *yoni,* he gains the merit of bathing at ten thousand *tirthas*. The forehead mark should be made from *yoni tattva*, and the dress should be of the Kaula type.

Firstly, in intercourse, the purified worshipper should draw the Shakti to himself by her hair and should place his *lingam* into her hand. The *lingam puja* and the *yoni puja* should be performed according to the injunctions. Beloved One, red powder and sandal should be smeared on the *lingam*. The *lingam* should be inserted into the *yoni* and there should be vigorous intercourse. After going to a cremation ground, offering cooked fish, milk, food and

meat, he becomes like Kubera, the God of Wealth. A *yantra* of *yoni* shape should be drawn on the ground and the mantra recited.

If one sees the *yoni* full of menses, after bathing and reciting the mantra 108 times, a person becomes a Shiva on earth. One should recite the mantra after offering both one's own semen and the *yoni* flowers. By all means a *sadhaka* should have intercourse in the *yoni*, caressing the Shakti's breasts. A *sadhaka* becomes instantly regenerated and fully alive by using the water from washing the *yoni* and *lingam*. The water of the *yoni* is of three types and one should offer it to the Shakti Mahadevi, after mixing the water with wine; a purified *sadhaka* should drink it. The highest *sadhaka* should mix the effusion from the *yoni* and *lingam* in water,

❋ Venerated for its obvious properties of fertility and growth, the *yoni* was seen as the centre of concentrated energy or *tejas* which when stimulated gave birth to all creation.

sipping this *amrita,* he should nourish himself with it.

Great Lady, listen very attentively. The miraculous *yoni tattva* Tantra is the best of all Tantras. The only evil in sexual intercourse is disgust for blood and semen. He who mixes them with wine is discriminating in worship. The *yoni* which has bled is suitable for worship. Do not worship a *yoni* which has never bled. Worshipping a *yoni* which has never bled causes loss of *siddhi* (psychic power) on every occasion.

The sin acquired in a myriad of births is instantly destroyed if one worships, offering oneself into the *yoni* aperture. Combining semen with menses or *svayambhu* menses and taking this in the hand, carefully offer it into the *yoni.*

✺ *Above:* In a number of Tantric texts, the woman as epitomized by Shakti is the dominant lover of a quiescent Shiva.

148

The *Mahavidya, mantra* and preparation of the *mantra* do not bestow *siddhi* without worship of the *yoni*. One should bow thrice before the *yoni* with a flower, Maheshvari, else the puja of a man is useless even in 1000 lifetimes. The best sort of *sadhaka* should have intercourse with all other *yonis*. Intoxicated, they laud and sing hymns in his praise. The greatest thing in mantra recitation and *sadhana* is the outflow of semen and vaginal emission.

Parvati said: 'Ocean of Compassion, by what method should the *yoni*, which is the essence of the cosmos, to be worshipped? If you or a *sadhaka* should worship a *yoni*, how does it bestow grace?'

Mahadeva said: 'A *sadhaka* wishing to worship a *yoni*, which is the form of the cosmos, should cause an erection and insert it into that thing which is Shakti Herself. The vagina is *Mahamaya* and the penis is *Sadashiva*.

'After reciting the mantra 100 times

✤ *Above:* 'Shiva and Shakti are recognized as being one and the same because consciousness cannot be separated from creative energy. Hence, Shiva without Shakti is a corpse.'

at the base of the *yoni,* one should rub the *lingam* and the *yoni* together.'

✤

'If a person should gaze at a *yoni* while ritually bathing, his life becomes fruitful. One should look at one's partner's *yoni,* at another woman's *yoni,* the *yoni* of a maiden—in the absence of a maiden's *yoni* one should gaze reverentially at the *yoni* of a pupil. Never worship the *yoni* in front of *pashus.* The wise man should always avoid blame, disgust or shame of the *yoni.*'

Tantric texts thus taught that everything had to be experienced playfully, but with awareness and a sense of sacredness. Channelized properly these experiences can provide an unparalleled source of energy, continually increasing ecstasy for the individual while simultaneously leading one to seek Supreme Consciousness. Another of these Tantra texts known as the *Gupta Sadhana Tantra,* written around the 13th century deals with the *sadhana* or worship of Shakti in 13 *patalas.* Some are mentioned below:

Set on the pleasant peak of Kailash Mountain, Devi says that she has heard of the greatness of the path of the *kulas* (an esoteric sect or community), but wants to know more. Shiva replies that *kulachara* (the learning of the *kulas*) is great knowledge and should be concealed, particularly from those who have a *pashu* (herdlike) disposition. He adds that the *kulashakti* (the female energy) should be worshipped with the five *makaras* (M-sounds), and describes the *shaktis* suitable for this worship as a dancer, a whore, a washerwoman, a girl who cuts hair, a *Brahmani* (an upper-caste woman), a *Shudrani* (a woman of low caste), and a flower girl.

These are some of the *kulashaktis.*

This chapter deals with Shakti and her characteristics. Shankara says that she may be one's own *shakti* or another's. She should be youthful and intelligent, and should be free of shame *(lajja)* and disgust *(ghrna).* After using the five elements according to the rule, the *sadhaka* should recite the mantra placing it 100 times on the head, 100 times on the forehead, 100 times where the hair is parted in the centre *(sinduramandala* or *simanta),* 100 times on the mouth, 100 times on the throat, 100 times in the region of the heart, 100 times for each of her breasts, 100 times for the navel, and 100 times at the *yoni.* After doing so, the *sadhaka* should think of himself as one with Shiva, and using the Shiva mantra should worship his own *lingam.* Chewing *tambula* (betel leaf), and with bliss or excitement in his heart, he should place his *lingam* in the *yoni* of Shakti. The semen which flows from this orgasm should then be offered to the Devi.

Tantric texts were not restricted to Hinduism alone and played an important role in Buddhism too. In India, Tantric

✤ *Facing page:* The conjunction of Shiva and Shakti expresses the sacredness of sexuality as a path to spiritual union epitomizing a symbolism of the social, sexual and sacred interconnectedness between woman, man and the cosmos.

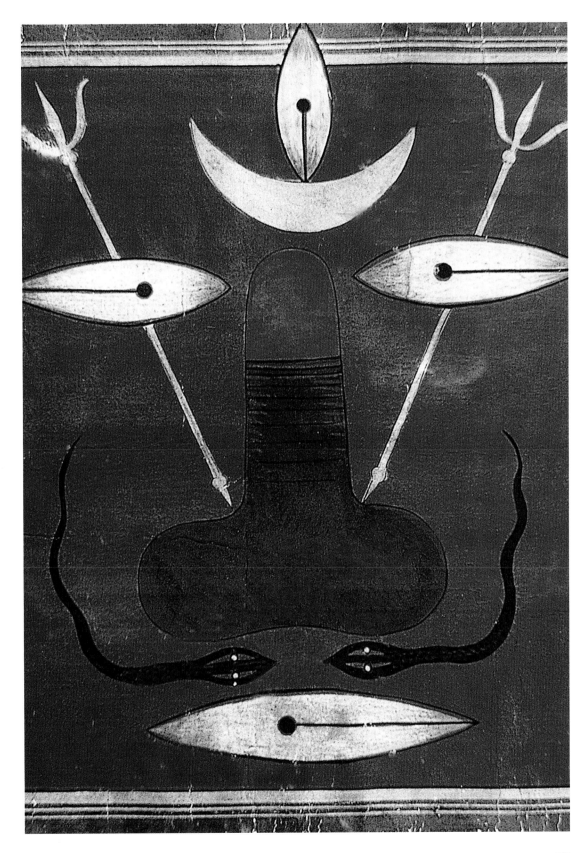

Buddhism probably began around 300 AD as an esoteric development among small circles of initiates, passed down from teacher to disciple. It gathered momentum after 600 AD, and was espoused by the rulers of a kingdom known as Uddyana (possibly around Peshawar in modern Pakistan) and by the Pala dynasty in Bengal (750-1150). According to its own historians, Buddhist Tantra known as Vajrayana, originates from the Shakyamuni Buddha and is said to have first been transmitted at the request of a king called Indrabuthi, who wished to practise *dharma* but was unwilling to give up his kingdom and queens, as was normally expected of Buddhist monks. Among Buddha's disciples, the bodhisattvas Vajrapani, Manjusri, and Avalokiteshvara were entrusted with Tantric teachings that were passed down in secrecy, teacher to disciple, for many centuries. One of these *mahasiddhas*, Guru Padmasambhava, travelled to Tibet, established Vajrayana as the state religion and initiated the first Tantric lineage in Tibet known as the Nyingma. Vajrayana eventually spread

❧ *Above:* Maithuna signifies sexual union which was to be performed keeping in mind that the idea behind the union was only a symbol for the union of the individual consciousness with the divine.

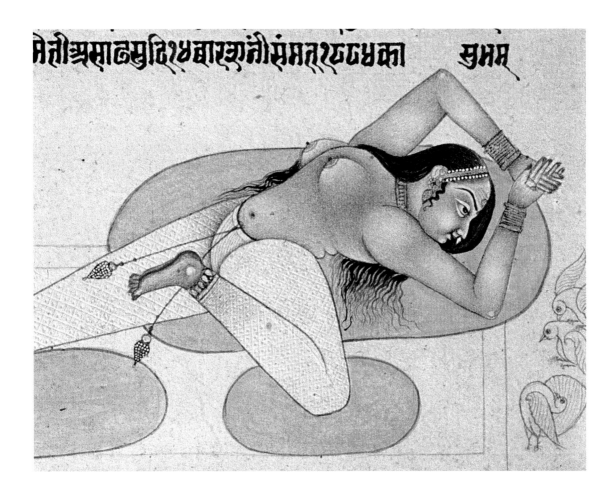

through Central Asia, into Mongolia and China, and as far as Japan.

The complete asceticism that was advocated in Buddhism appears to have undergone complete reversal in Tantric Buddhism. The contempt for the world of senses, the degradation of women as well as the asexuality appears to have turned on its head resulting in an explosion of sexuality embedded in the idea that sexual love harbours the secret of the universe. Here too the erotic encounter between man and woman is granted a mystical aura and vested with an authority and power completely denied in previous Buddhist dogma. Thus in the Vajrayana sect, every feminine experience is exalted enjoying respect and high esteem.

'Women are heaven; women are *dharma*; ... women are Buddha; women are the *sangha*; women are the perfection of wisdom...'
—*Candamaharosana Tantra*

❊ *Above:* 'I have visited in my wanderings shrines and other places of pilgrimage, But I have not seen another shrine blissful like my own body.'

cittavisuddhiprakarana

As if taking its cue from Hindu Tantrism, in Vajrayana too sexuality becomes the event, the life-force upon which all else is based—not for its own sake but to achieve *Nirvana* (liberation). Sexual indulgence was seen as a path to liberation as extolled in these two passages from the seventh-century *Cittavisuddhiprakarana* of Aryadeva:

liberation
through indulgence

I have visited in my wanderings shrines and
　　other places of pilgrimage,
But I have not seen another shrine blissful like
　　my own body.
Eat and drink, indulge the senses,
Fill the *mandala* (with offerings) again and
　　again,
By things like these you'll gain the world beyond.

Enjoying the world of sense, one is undefiled
　　by the world of sense.
One plucks the lotus without touching the
　　water.
So the *yogin* who has gone to the root of
　　things
Is not enslaved by the senses although he
　　enjoys them.
Even as water entering water
Has the same saviour,
So faults and virtues are accounted the same
As there is no opposition between them.

The supreme bliss of orgasm

There is neither passion nor absence of
　　passion.
Seated beside her own, her mind destroyed,
Thus I have seen the *yogini*.
That blissful delight that exists between the
　　lotus (vagina) and *vajra* (thunderbolt, *i.e.,*
　　penis),
Who does not rejoice there?
This moment may be the bliss of means, or of
　　both wisdom and means...
It is profound, it is vast.
It is neither self nor other...
Even as the moon makes light in black
　　darkness,
So in one moment the supreme bliss removes
　　all defilement.
When the sun of suffering has set,
Then arises this bliss, this lord of the stars.
It creates with continuous creativity,
And of this comes the *mandala* (of the
　　cosmos).
Gain purification in bliss supreme,
For here lies final perfection.

Another text known as the *Guhyasamaja Tantra*, which loosely translates as the 'assembly of secrets' is probably the earliest and most important of Buddhist Tantric scriptures. This treatise, represents one of the root texts that were instrumental in the development of Vajrayana and states that, if *siddhis* are to be acquired, women must always be an integral part of this quest. The text speaks of the virtues inherent in desire and sensory enjoyment, the well-being of body and mind, and of realizing the 'Buddha nature' through the union of female and male. It differs from many later texts in not condemning male ejaculation but says that:

When the diamond (*i.e., lingam*) is connected to the lotus (*i.e., yoni*) in the union of both polarities, one worships the Buddhas and the diamond beings with the drops of one's semen.

This text also allows for sexual union between siblings and between mother with son, indicating that even within the fold of Buddhism with its unequivocal prohibition of 'adultery', incest, and its demand for continence, Tantra preserved its radical element:

Do not suppress your feelings,
choose whatever you will,

✽ *Above, left:* Tantrics believe in spiritual empowerment through the celebration of sexual energy.
Right: A Tantric Hanuman is perceived as the paragon of spiritual power.

and do whatever you desire,
for in this way you please the
Goddess.
No one succeeds in attaining
perfection
by employing difficult and vexing
operations;
but perfection can be gained
by satisfying all one's desires
says the *Prajnopaya Viniscaya Siddhi.*

Ultimately, whatever route the seeker or *sadhaka* follows within the various tantric paths, they were all designed to help merge oneself with the divine. This is the reason Tantra never tires of repeating that everything can be an opportunity for enlightenment. Tantra, in fact, is not just about experiencing uplifting experiences but recognizes and includes even disturbing emotions. It recognizes that divinity is all pervasive and dwells not just in love but in lust, in happiness and in sorrow, in equanimity and anger and every other emotion that makes us human beings. The attempt is to recognize, accept and ultimately transcend each of these emotions so that we do not remain trapped and held hostage by them.

✤ *Facing page and above:* 'Do not suppress your feelings, choose whatever you will, do whatever you desire, for in this way you please the Goddess.'

shiva and parvati

Only when Shiva is united with Shakti does he have the power to create.
—*Saundarya Lahiri*

The three main components of Hindu Tantra without which it cannot exist are Shiva, Shakti and Jiva where Shiva represents Supreme Consciousness from which emanated the Shaiva cults, Shakti the agent through which this Consciousness manifests itself and is known as the Shakta *marga* or path, and Jiva is the individual person and the identity of the self. Ancient philosophers believed that the world or reality as they called it is made up of two fundamental principles: Shiva, the Absolute One in its own essential, perfect, unchanging, non-dual consciousness nature; and Shakti, which is that Absolute One's own power of self-manifestation. Existing from the earliest times, pre-dating the advent of the Aryans into the Indian subcontinent, this idea of Shiva is one of the oldest human experiences and expressions of God, often depicted as the Lord of Creation and Destruction, as *Sat-Chit-Ananda*, the purveyor of all that is True, Conscious and Blissful.

Among the primitive herdsmen and early agriculturists, the act of generation was considered as no more than an aspect of nature contributing to the reproduction of the species, as in agriculture the sowing of seed, and the magical method of seemingly creating out of nothing was consequently looked upon as sacred. In those early ages, all the functions of nature were consecrated to some divinity. Thus in Egypt, the act of generation was consecrated to Khem; in Assyria, to Vul; in the Greek pastoral ages to Pan; and in later times, to Priapus. Among the Mexicans, the God of Generation was named Triazoltenti. These gods became the representatives of the generative or fructifying powers in man and nature. In India this creative energy came to be known as Shiva and came to be symbolically represented as the *lingam* or phallus—a rather stylized symbol which stands for an eternal column of light, the purest form of godhood.

The story of Shiva is fragmented. Historians and Indologists trace the beginnings of the idea of Shiva to very early in history as the deity of the Harappan civilization. Variously known as Maheshvara, the Great Lord, Mahadeva, the Great God, Hara (Lord), Pinakadhrik or Bearer of the Axe and Mrityunjaya, Conqueror of Death, Shiva is ironically both Creator and

Destroyer, the Conqueror of Lust and Desire, and is also known as the erotic ascetic.

Shakti on the other hand is the feminine creative aspect of Shiva and is often depicted as Shiva's consort. Though not interchangeable, Shiva and Shakti were recognized as being one and the same because consciousness cannot be separated from creative energy—without the power to manifest there could be no creation. As the Bengal Shakta Tantrics say: 'Shiva without Shakti is a corpse,' *i.e.,* lifeless, inert. This life-giving force is to this day worshipped as Shakti. This principle of oneness or non-duality came to be described in the Tantric texts as *maithuna* or sexual intercourse. One Tantric text the *Kama-kala-vilasa* describes Shiva or Mahesha as pure illumination or self-shining with all the principles of activity contracted within it. This conjunction of Shiva and Shakti expresses the sacredness of sexuality as a path to spiritual union epitomizing a symbolism of the social, sexual and sacred interconnectedness between man, woman and the cosmos.

The mythologies surrounding Shiva are immense for the story of Shiva goes back many millennia. Shiva today is a composite god becoming more or less what you want him to be, as in him all contradictions coexist. The usual depiction of Shiva as an ascetic living on the fringes of society was not because he had rejected it but because he had transcended it. There are countless stories on the genesis of his symbolic representation as a *lingam* or phallus, but none more telling than the one found in the *Shiva Purana.*

The *Puranas* are enormously influential texts in the popular religious expressions of Hindu India. These are essentially regarded to be sacred works and are a collection of laws, tales, and a philosophy that reflect the teachings of older scriptures. There are eighteen *Maha Puranas*, all written in verse and varying in length from about 10,000–81,000 couplets. Represented as being divinely transmitted, they usually take the form of a dialogue between an interpreter and an inquirer. The best known of these are the *Shiva Purana, Skanda Purana*, and *Linga Purana,* all considered to be the holy scriptures of Shaivism. The *puranic* canon is of prime importance in understanding the genesis of phallus worship:

the emergence of the lingam

The sages enquired: 'How did the pre-eminence of the *lingam*, exclusive of Shiva, come to be established?'

Lomasa said: 'Lord Shambhu (another name for Shiva) wandered about in the forest Daruvana begging for alms. At midday when the sages went to the holy river for a bath, the wives of these sages gathered together on seeing Sambhu. "Who is this personage of uncommon appearance?"

'So saying, they went home and gathering various kinds of alms, offered it to Lord Shiva with due honour and gentleness. One of the ladies, struck with wonder and attracted to Shambhu said: "Who are you? Why have you come here as a mendicant?"

❈ *Facing page:* Shiva as Nataraja represents sustenance, destruction, veiling, salutation and grace. The circle of fire signifies not only a destructive force but an equally potent purifying and regenerative one.

'Shambhu replied:"I am bereaved of Daksayani and hence I wander about nude for the purpose of begging alms, O Lady of excellent hips. I am free from any wish or desire or any expectation of advantage from anybody. O Beautiful Lady, without Sati all the women in the world do not at all appeal to me."

'On hearing this, the lotus-eyed lady said: "There is no doubt that women can give pleasure by their mere touch. You have eschewed such pleasurable women!" Thus all the young women gathered around him forsaking their domestic duties, their minds dwelling on him alone.

'When the sages returned to their hermitages and found their homes vacant, they searched for their wives. Thereupon they saw them following Shiva. On seeing Shambu the sages angrily closed in upon him cursing him: "Since you are the abductor of our wives, you shall instantaneously become a eunuch."

'Cursed by the sages, Lord Shiva's penis immediately fell down to the ground and as it touched the ground, it grew larger and larger increasing enormously in size covering the seven *patalas* pervading the entire earth and heavens. There was no earth, no quarter, neither water nor fire, neither wind nor ether, neither Cosmic Ego *(ahmkara)* nor the Great Principle *(mahat)*, neither the Unmanifest One

✴ 'O Spouse of Shiva, Mother of mine, assuming the form of the ripples of Kalindi on Thy slim waist, you appear to the enlightened; the attenuated ether intervening the two pot-like breasts entering the hole of Thy navel, owing to the pressing each of the two breasts.'

(avyakta) nor the Time and no great Primordial Matter *(prakrti)*. Since the entire universe became *lina* (merged) in that *lingam* (phallus) of the great Atman, it came to be called so.'

The female principle on the other hand has been worshipped in an unbroken lineage that goes back thousands of years. All over India monuments dating from as early as 6000 to 2000 BC symbolize the great active power in the universe, Shakti. Assimilated into Hindu mythology, the Devi or Goddess became not merely the consort of a male god but a supreme power unto herself. Mother-Goddess figurines with exaggerated buttocks and breasts are prolific for just as Shiva was depicted as the energy or phallus, Shakti is symbolized as the *yoni* or the primordial womb from which all things emanate and into which all things return. Thus the *Shakti Sangama Tantra* says:

> Woman is the creator of the universe,
> the universe is her form;
> woman is the foundation of the world,
> she is the true form of the body.
> In woman is the form of all things,
> of all that lives and moves in the world.
> There is no jewel rarer than woman, no
> condition superior to that of a woman.
> No wonder even the most powerful of
> gods, like Shiva above, crave to enter the
> feminine form, hoping to acquire at least
> some of her glorious power.

Thus from the earliest times, the divine feminine was called Shakti signifying the ultimate primordial creative power. The word

is derived from the Sanskrit root word '*shak*', meaning potency or the potential to produce. All interpretations of the word hold common one parameter, namely power—more specifically the power to create. Shakti represents the fundamental creative instinct underlying the cosmos and the energizing force behind all divinity. Expressed in a myriad ways, she is variously represented as the consort of Lord Shiva, she is an independent goddess or devi, she is also the *yoni* or vulva. The re-emergence of the tradition of the Great Goddess cults after several centuries of a patriarchal pantheon further nurtured the Tantric movement giving rise to significant literature and poetics like the *Saundarya Lahiri*. The *Samkara Bhagavatpada* widely known as the *Saundarya Lahiri* or the Ocean of Beauty is simultaneously, a poem in the finest tradition of Sanskrit poetics, a mantra that contains mystic formulae as well as an exposition of Agama and Tantra worship. This *strotra* or hymn is a rather vivid description of the Supreme Being as Shakti, the creative energy. An independent goddess, devi or Durga is often shown adorned with weapons, poised for battle but always a picture of supreme beauty. Believed to be composed by Shankara, India's greatest Advaita philosopher, the *Saudarya Lahiri* is a vividly sensuous paean to the goddess:

> Having adored Thee,
> the   bestower   of

✤ Lord Shiva depicted as a *lingam* or phallus symbolizing the creative energies of the cosmos.

prosperity to those that made the obeisance before Thee, Hari, of yore, assumed the form of a damsel and fascinated even the destroyer of the (three) Puras. Likewise, by worshipping Thee, is powerful enough to rouse the passion of even great sages, with a (charming) frame fit to be licked by Rati's eyes.

Damsels in hundreds, with their locks dishevelled, their saris flying off their figures, their girdles bursting asunder with force, their silk garments slipping down, run after a decrepit, ugly and impotent man, who falls within the range of Thy side-glances.

How many among the celestial courtesans, including Urvasi, with the shy eyes of the timid wild deer, would not be caught in the clutches of him, who conceives the entire Heaven and Earth submerged in the red radiance caused by the lustrous graces of Thy body, forming, as it were, the abodes of the splendors of the rising sun.

O Spouse of Shiva, Mother of mine, assuming the form of the ripples of Kalindi on Thy slim waist, you appear to the enlightened; the attenuated ether intervening the two pot-like breasts entering the hole of Thy navel, owing to the pressing each of the two breasts.

O Parvati! The King of the Mountains bestowed on Thee by way of dowry heaviness and vastness taken out of his flanks. Hence, these, Thy prodigious hips, being both broad and heavy, hide from view the entire terrestrial world and make it light as well.

O Daughter of the Mountain! Having surpassed the trunks of lordly elephants and the clusters of golden plantain stumps with Thy two thighs, Thou hast likewise surpassed their pair of frontal globes of the divine elephant with Thy pair of perfectly rounded knees, hardened by constant prostration before Thy Lord.

With the idea of the feminine taking such strong roots, the Shakti cults saw the active participation of women in rituals unlike the completely male-dominated ceremonies prescribed by Vedic scriptures. The Shakta in Tantra especially, could not conduct any ritual without his wife who was regarded as his Shakti. For enlightenment, it was believed, could only be achieved by the union of Shiva and Shakti. The underpinning idea behind all this symbolism is the Hindu precept that divinity resides in each one of us, that all of us have been endowed with inherent powers that have to be tapped, its potential realized. The purpose of this ritualized coupling as it were, was not mere physical union, nor was it to fulfill lust or to procreate. Rather this was yet another pathway leading to perfect Bliss or Supreme Reality.

❋ *Facing page:* The Shakti cults saw the active participation of women for ritual coupling not merely to satiate lust or to procreate, but as being part of a pathway to the Supreme Reality.

conclusion

Follow your bliss. Find where it is, and don't be afraid to follow it.
—Joseph Campbell, *The Power of Myth*

the idea that life has meaning and that for the most part its purpose is the pursuit of happiness is an accepted creed in most societies both ancient and modern. Happiness has meant all things to all people but the fundamental definition as the achievement of the highest good for oneself remains the same even as the shifting sands of values and traditions, societal concepts of good and bad, commerce and global economics irrevocably keep changing its quality.

This eternal quest for illusive happiness and contentment has resulted in tremendous achievements this last century—more than what mankind has been able to achieve in the last 4000 years. Material progress and scientific advancement have made ours the healthiest, most comfortable and intellectually superior generation that has inhabited this planet, yet there is no greater joy or peace than there was in the past. More than ever before, life now revolves around the quest for happiness as emanating from wealth, power, satisfactory relationships or sexual well-being. This pursuit becomes an end in itself and oftentimes, despite achieving the required results, there is still a

❋ *Facing page:* 'From bliss did things come into being. In bliss do they exist and to bliss do they return finally.'

persistent dissatisfaction, a lingering sense of pain and anxiety. So, while modern man has at his command his creature comforts, the voice within struggles to comprehend the extent of his all-pervasive unhappiness.

Reflecting this, Buddhism believes that this world is full of *dukha* or misery. According to the Buddha, everything—birth, life, death and the world is *dukha*. Furthermore, everything is also seen as being *kshanika* or momentary. According to Buddhism therefore, only on achieving the state of *Nirvana*, which translates as liberation or oblivion, can this misery end. On the other hand, while Hinduism believes that the constant pursuit of happiness dependent on the external world will bring only sorrow, it also affirms that life is *ananda* or bliss. 'From bliss did things come into being. In bliss do they exist, and to bliss do they return finally,' say the Vedas.

Hinduism believes that the natural state of man is one of bliss; and as no man will voluntarily seek to be unhappy—*dukha* is an unnatural state of being. Sorrow is not natural to us; what is natural is happiness and its pursuit. However, as civilizations have evolved and changed, the concept of happiness has become increasingly

materialistic—the pursuit of joy emanating from outside oneself. Any external search for happiness would fail and only lead to unhappiness and misery. Recognizing this, most philosophies across the world have categorized happiness into two kinds: temporal and permanent. Temporal happiness, like the Buddhist concept of *kshanika* is what appears in our conscious existence for a limited period of time, providing momentary glimpses of how joyous life could be; permanent happiness on the other hand is without intermittent episodes of unhappiness or *dukha*. Hindu thought has always warned against the impermanence of material comforts believing it to be momentary and recommends the need to look within. Marrying Hindu religiosity and western materialism is a challenge not only for Indians but for all societies as the quest for a better, happier, more balanced version of ourselves and the lives we lead becomes a universal phenomenon.

Sages believed that this *ananda* or even the awareness of a state of bliss lay within

✽ *Above:* Coitus is the ultimate principle behind creation, preservation and destruction of the universe.

the reach of every human being, and is an intrinsic aspect of human existence. The purpose of men therefore becomes to realize this and rise from a lower level of consciousness and seek a higher plane of being—to rise from animality to divinity. Friedrich Nietzsche, the 19th-century German philosopher who declared that God was dead, often compared human beings to a rope stretched between an animal and a deity. Thus the dynamics of reconciliation between the physical, biological and emotional needs of human

beings as well as the equally valid aspirations to evolve into a higher being is a crucial part of all moral, religious, and spiritual traditions of the world.

The ideal of everlasting joy or bliss has been explored rather extensively by Hindu sages who understood the various aspects of life and its attractions and came to the rather modern conclusion that for human beings to realize their full potential, using the tangible energies of their own mind, body and intellect was better than resorting to the often esoteric and mystical systems of

❋ *Above:* The same cosmic energy that created the world is present in living beings as the sex force which is regarded as sacred, worthy of worship and not to be frittered away.

thought that form Indian scriptural work. Tapping into these energies meant tapping into one's own abilities and powers which in turn transformed human beings making them more conscious, rational as well as sexually aware beings. Towards this end, Hinduism evolved a system of thought that advocated action—a physical, mental and spiritual discipline that incorporated meditation, yoga, and sacramental worship in the widest sense of the term.

Thus developed sciences like yoga, based on the belief that human happiness and contentment arose from the perfect synchronization between a strong body and a clear mind. Developed by the sage Patanjali around 200 BCE, yoga encompasses several techniques that move beyond the body and mind, help withdraw from the physical world to focus on the inner, spiritual life that in its final stages approaches the state of Pure Being known as *Sat-Chit-Ananda*. Yoga developed as a science of holistic living, going well beyond merely the physical consisting of techniques that transform the mind, body and intellect while providing a comprehensive philosophy for leading an integrated life. Defined by Sri Aurobindo as the Art of Conscious Self Finding, yoga like the concepts of *bhakti*, or even Tantra was another way to expand the limits of our consciousness to gain mastery of the mind. Recognizing that the mind was the cause of most bondage leading to trauma and unhappiness, yoga provided the means to master the mind. What it teaches is concentration, the ability to focus attention on any given subject or

object as well as meditation which is the ability to quieten one's mind at will. Believing that a still mind is pure spirit, yoga provides yet another path in the search for bliss.

Parallel to this ran the understanding that in order to attain this state of *ananda* or even a modicum of peace and happiness in life, what was essential was motivation. Desire or motivation is intrinsic to Hindu thought where even creation has been symbolized as having emanated from God's head as Kamadeva or the God of Desire. This desire or urge to seek and unite with the divine was understood to be no less passionate and intense than the desire of two lovers to come together. '*Maithunam paramam tatvam, shrushti stithi anya karanam…*(Coitus is the ultimate principle behind creation, preservation and destruction of the universe),' says Lord Shiva in the *Kailash Tantra*. The belief that the same cosmic energy that created the world is present in living beings as the sex force is what led Hindus to regard this energy as something sacred, worthy of worship and not to be frittered away.

Indian religious thought has always recognized the parallel between sexuality and spirituality. And whether modern society accepts the ideal of sexuality as intrinsic to human beings as it did in the past or spends its time rejecting and attempting to control the sexual urges of its population, sex has been and remains a pivotal and primordial vital force, its impact on our lives and culture being both profound and inescapable. Sexuality in the

❋ *Facing page:* Hinduism evolved a system of thought that advocated action on several levels—physical, mental and spiritual discipline in the pursuit of a holistic existence.

171

past had been seen as a lawful, if limited expression of bliss but more importantly as a means of getting in touch with a higher consciousness. This sex-positive spiritual view holds that to truly become whole, we must liberate our sexuality from the chains of guilt, shame and repression, and allow it to find full expression as a natural, healthy and even sacred part of life.

We live in times when it is important to understand and confront sexuality and all its attendant emotions rather than to resort to the centuries-old habit of repression. For as

surely as it divides human beings into widely differing aspects, it also unifies them through their intrinsic urge to seek the other and become whole. Within sex lies the quest for the mystical, the mysteries of the universe and of existence itself, for in it lies the promise of endless regeneration, of eternal life. Osho says it best:

Sex is man's most vibrant energy, but it should not be an end unto itself. Sex should lead man to his soul. The goal is from lust to light. Not from

❈ *Preceding pages 172-173:* The desire to unite with the divine was considered to be no less intense than the desire of two lovers to unite.

❈ *Above;* A high level of aesthetic sensitivity prevailed in ancient India, a sensitivity that was charged with imagination and sensuality, a world view in which life was a celebration.

sex to superconsciousness, sex is superconsciousness. There is no higher, no lower.

Thus while western societies and philosophies have for long seen sex as the enemy of the spirit, the ancient Hindus saw it as an ally—a concept that has rapidly gained expediency in the past 50 years as modern physicists come to the conclusion that what exists in nature is not solid matter but energy. Psychologists from Freud onwards too have conceded that the sexual drive and its inbuilt energy can be sublimated into higher avenues such as aesthetics and spirituality. 'The elements of the sexual instinct are characterized by a capacity for sublimation, for changing their sexual aim into another of a different kind and socially more worthy. To the sum of energies thus gained for our psychological productions we probably owe the highest results of our culture,' wrote Freud. A fact recognized by ancient Asian philosophers who went so far as to attribute the development of the fine arts

✽ *Above:* A relationship between a man and a woman was treated with artistic finesse where every nuance of the romantic emotion was tastefully expressed and gracefully experienced.

✤ 'O my slender beauty, You, whom even the snakes could not frighten on the way, Now tremble at the mere touch of my arm.'

❋ 'The man who has virility should cohabit with a woman.
So, come near and unite with me.'

and even civilized society to the sexual impulse.

Be that as it may the real challenge and one of the most intimidating tasks before modern beings is the integration of this sexual impulse with spirituality. The split that has arisen by social conditioning and cultural training that makes love the highest of emotions, and sex a bad word has not just to be reconciled but in the words of ancient Indians 'unified'. The belief that the body, mind and soul were an integrated whole, that every aspect of life had to be explored, understood and lived to potential has been the bedrock of Hindu philosophy with its concept of its four aims of life or *purusharthas—dharma*, *artha*, *kama* and *moksha*. Religion serves to rein in desire progressively from ephemeral pleasures to seek ultimate bliss. It is a process of gaining maturity and wisdom to forsake the smaller pleasures for the ultimate bliss of *moksha*. Seen in this order, Indians believe that the purpose of life in the material realm is to work out our material as well as physical desires, and to rise above them and reach a point in which every aspect of life, be it challenges or reversals, misfortunes or successes, joys or sorrows, become avenues of discovering who we are. Thus if a righteous life was good, so was the pursuit of wealth as was the quest for a sexually fulfilling life.

Paradoxically corresponding to the belief that life could be energized by adopting a sensual yet controlled sex life, was the ideal of asceticism. In India there appears to be no contradiction in accepting both sexuality

❋ The belief was that the quality of living could be enhanced by adopting a sensual but controlled sexual life.

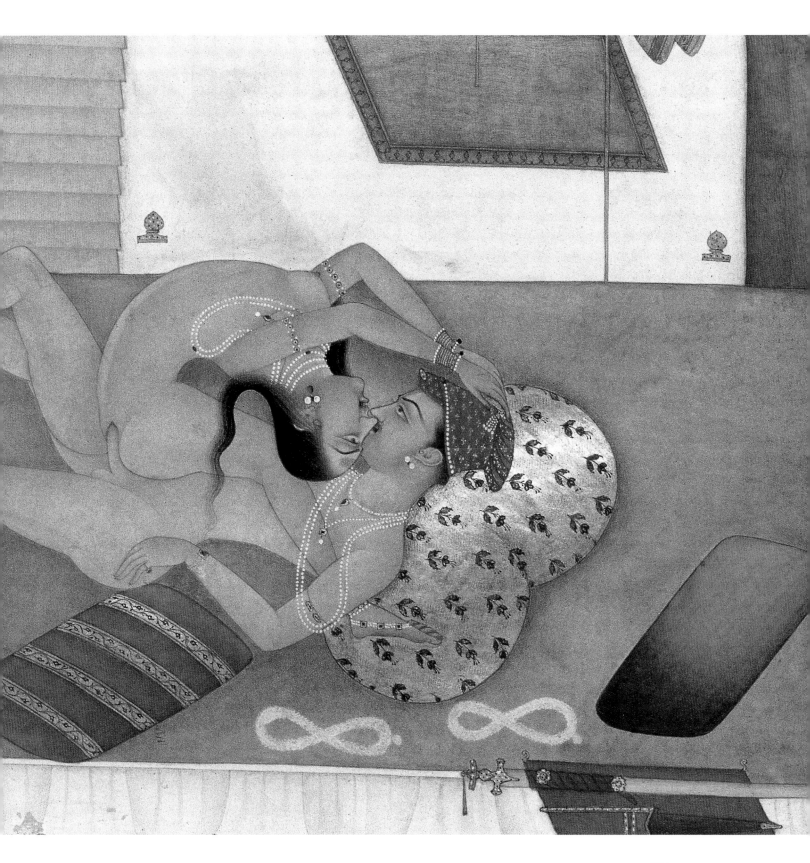

and celibacy as accepted pathways to the divine. In Hindu mythology, this paradox between the ascetic and the erotic, between desire (*kama*) and detachment (*vyragya*), between birth and death, is best illustrated by the myth of the burning of Kamadeva by Lord Shiva. Shiva's resolve to remain an ascetic was considered inimical to the continuity of life, yet Kama had to distract him, for without love there could be no life. The dichotomy was thus resolved not by denying the existence of sensuality or the importance of sexual pleasure but by sublimating it into a transcendent, blissful state.

For instance, the *Rg Veda* records a domestic quarrel between a renowned ascetic called Agastya and his wife Lopamudra. Their quarrel, of course, was over sex or rather the lack thereof. Lopamudra complains to her husband,

> Many years have I been serving thee diligently, both day and night through dawn up to an old age. Decay now impairs the beauty of my limbs, what, therefore, is now to be done? Shouldn't husbands' approach their wives? The man who has virility should cohabit with a woman. So, come near and unite with me.

Lopamudra thus demands her husband's attention and being sufficiently experienced in the art of seduction, slowly entices the otherwise disinclined and reluctant sage to succumb to her womanly wiles.

Why has this rather intimate conversation between a husband and wife found its way into the most ancient and venerated of Hindu texts? Most accept the fact of its existence to mean that sexuality and asceticism were not contradictory, rather two aspects of the same coin—which was the quest of the divine.

Resolution of this dichotomy is a battle that has been fought by men and women ever since religions began to spread the idea that in order to seek a spiritual life one must curb the passions of the flesh. Entire traditions have arisen based on this mistaken ideology namely that communion with the divine depended on repressing or confining sexual urge. Complete renunciation of sex was the grand ideal to which countless ascetics in ancient India aspired. While there are a few instances of sages who were able to withstand the force of Kamadeva, many more are remembered for failing to uphold this supreme ideal. For example, in the Ramayana, the illustrious sage Vishvamitra's passion becomes enflamed when he sees the celestial nymph Menaka bathing in a stream near his hermitage. His love affair with her lasts for a full ten years, at which point he comes to his senses and resumes a doubly fierce ascetic life. Similarly Sharadvant a mighty yogi and skilled archer on seeing a scantily clad maiden temporarily loses control over his mind and involuntarily drops his bow, arrows and semen.

For the ascetic, lust was an ally of death, for loss of semen signalled loss of power, energy, and hard-earned *punya* or merit. The

❋ *Facing page:* In Hindu mythology, this paradox between the ascetic and the erotic, is resolved not by denying the existence of sensuality but by sublimating it into a transcendent, blissful state.

ascetic needed the body's energy to accomplish the task of self-transformation that is the goal of all austerities. It was believed that abstinence was essential to convert sexual energy (*retas*) into spiritual energy (*tejas*). And that when a person controls his sexual impulse, his energy changes direction and goes up through the back of his spine activating his higher *chakras* or centres of spiritual energy. Ancient Hindus firmly believed that being celibate was essential to reach the world of Brahman. Swami Chidananda, the revered president of the Divine Life Society, says: '*Brahmacharya*, or celibacy, is a rational process of preserving and conserving precious energy so that it can be utilized in other very essential and indispensable functions. And if preserved it can be converted, just as gross water is converted into subtle steam.'

As the world turns increasingly to ancient wisdom in its search for wholeness, peace and happiness, the central and recurring theme in most ancient philosophies and disciplines is the need to banish negativity and excesses, the need to look beyond ourselves and see the whole of which we are a part. All spiritual texts teach an art that helps explore the hidden dimensions of the unity of the body and the mind one step at a time. Spiritual identity is the underlying principle of unity among all living entities, our task being to realign our consciousness to see this unity between all human beings and awakening this energy. And innumerable are the paths leading to this. Since there are temperamental differences among the individual seekers of truth, Hinduism recognizes the need for a variety of spiritual disciplines or *sadhanas* that give ordinary men and women the independence and choice to follow any route they want, to realize their material and physical desires before progressing towards spiritual progress. Call it love, worship, selfless devotion, service and compassion or call it Bhakti Yoga, Jnana Yoga, Karma Yoga, Kama Yoga or Tantra; they are paths to perfection, roads to realization of the truth that all lead to the same divine energy which is the Godhead. As the Upanishads say: '*Ekam sath viprah bahudha vadanti*—The truth is one, but the wise refer to it by various names.'

❋ *Facing page:* Spiritual identity is the underlying principle of unity among all living beings and our task is to realign our consciousness to see this ideal that is known as *Sat-Chit-Ananda.*

❋ *Following pages 184-185:* Love is truth, and truth is one, but described variously.

BIBLIOGRAPHY

Allen, Roger et al. (eds.), *Love and Sexuality in Modern Arabic Literature*, London, Saqi Books, 1995.

Anand, D. Krishna, *The Living God of Braj*, Abhinav Publications, New Delhi, 1992.

Anand, Subhash, *The Way of Love—The Bhagavata Doctrine of Bhakti*, New Delhi, 1996.

Arberry, A.J: *Farid al-Din Attar, Episodes from the Tadhkirat al-Auliya ('Memorial of the Saints')*, Penguin Group, UK.

Archer, William G., *The Loves of Krishna*, Grove Press, New York, 1957.

Avalon, Arthur (ed.), Tantrik Texts: *Kalivilasa Tantra*, Luzac and Co., London, 1917.

Avalon, Arthur, *The Great Liberation: Mahanirvana Tantra*, Ganesh and Co., Madras, 1913.

Ayyar Swaminathan U.V. Dr. (trans.) *Ainkurunuru*, South India Saiva Siddhanta Works Pub. Society, Madras, *c.* 1968.

Barbara Stoller Miller (ed. and trans.), *The Love Song of the Dark Lord: Jayadeva's Gitagovindam*, Columbia University Press, New York, 1977.

Bhattacharya, Deben (trans.) *Love Songs of Chandidas: The Rebel Poet-Priest of Bengal*, Grove Press, New York, *c.* 1970.

Bhattacharya, Deben (trans.), *Love Songs of Vidyapati*. Ed. with notes and introduction by W.G. Archer, London, 1963; reprint ed., Motilal Banarsidass, Delhi, 1987.

Burton Richard, Arbuthnot, F.F. (trans.) *Ananga Ranga by Kalyanamalla*, Oriental Paperbacks, New Delhi.

Candamaharosana Tantra, Harvard Oriental Series, Harvard University Press, 1976.

Chittick C. William, *The Self-Disclosure of God: Principles of Ibn Al-'Arabi's Cosmology*, SUNY Series in Islam, State University of New York Press, 1997.

Comfort, Dr. Alex, *The Kokashastra*, Preface by W.G. Archer, Simon and Schuster. New York, *c.* 1997.

Çre Govardhana Bhaooa Goswami—A Vine of Spring Pastimes. Translated by Advaita Dasa, 1989.

Danielou, Alain, *The Complete Kama Sutra:* The First Unabridged Modern Translation, Inner Traditions International, Vermont, USA.

Das Advaita (trans.) *Rasa Prabhanda-Prabodhananda* by Saraswati Goswami–Brindavan.

Dehejia, Harsha, *The Flute and the Lotus: Romantic Moments in Indian Poetry and Painting*, Mapin publishing, Ahmedabad, 2002.

Delmonico Neal and Aditi Nath (trans.) *Sri Krsna Kirtan*, 'How to Partake in the Love of Krishna,' in *Religions of India in Practice*, *c.* 1983.

Delmonico, Neal, (trans.) *Krishna Bhavanamrita*, Vishvanatha Chakravarti.

Devchar C.R., *Amarusatakam* and *Srngaradipika* of Vemabhupala: *A Centum of Ancient Love Lyrics*, Motilal Banarsidass, New Delhi.

Dimock Jr., E. and L. David, *In Praise of Krishna Songs from the Bengali*, London, *c.* 1967.

Douglas, Nik and Penny Slinger, *Sexual Secrets: The Alchemy of Ecstasy*, Destiny Books, New York, 1979.

Dupre, A., P. Young: *The Life and Influence of Ibn 'Arabi*, Proceedings of The First Annual Symposium of the Muhyiddin Ibn 'Arabi Society, Durham University, April 1984.

George, Christopher. S. *The Candamaharosana Tantra: A Critical Edition and English Translation*. Published Ph.D. dissertation, New Haven: American Oriental Series, 1974.

Gupta Sadhana Tantra at Dhyanasanjivini.org

Hart III, George L. (trans.), *Poets of the Tamil Anthologies: Ancient Poems of Love and War,* Princeton, N.J. Princeton University Press, *c.* 1979.

Jha, Subhadra, *The Songs of Vidyapati*, Benares, 1954.

Kale M.R., *Kumarasambhava of Kalidasa*, Motilal Banarsidass, New Delhi,1995.

Kinsley, David R., *The Divine Player (A Study of Krsna Lila)*, Motilal Banaridass, New Delhi, 1979.

Knapp Stephen, Essay: *The Meaning of the Phrase 'God is Love'*@ stephen-knapp.com

Knysh D. Alexander D., *Ibn 'Arabi in the Later Islamic Tradition—The making of a polemical image in medieval Islam,* SUNY Press, 1999.

Krishnadasa Kaviraja Goswami *Caitanya-caritamrta,* 9 Vols., *The Pastimes of Lord Chaitanya Mahaprabhu,* Brindavan.

Lee Seigel, translation of *Amarushatakam, Sacred and Profane Dimensions of Love in Indian Traditions,* Oxford University Press, Delhi, 1978 .

Loknath Maharaj and Mike Mcgee (trans.) *Yoni Tantra.* Reproduced here with permission.

Mohanta Sambaru Chandra (trans) *Ratnasara,* Benaras.

Mookerjee, Ajit, *Kali, The Feminine Force,* London, 1995.

Mulchandani, Sandhya (trans.), *Manmatha Samhita in Kama: The Romance of Desire,* India Research Press, Delhi, 2005.

Mulchandani, Sandhya (trans.), *Pururavasamanasijasutram Kama: The Romance of Desire,* India Research Press, Delhi, 2005.

Nitin Kumar, 'Awakening the Inner Woman Bhakti and the doctrine of Love.' Essay in exoticartindia.com

O'Flaherty, Wendy D., *The Origins of Evil in Hindu Mythology*, University of California Press.

'Ottoman Empire,' Encyclopædia Britannica, 2003. Encyclopædia Britannica Online.

Patterson Stephen and Marvin Meyer (trans.) *The Gospel of Thomas,* Gnostic Texts.

Quataert, Donald, *The Ottoman Empire, 1700-1922,* Cambridge, Cambridge University Press, 2000.

Rajneesh, Bhagwan (Osho), *Sex to Super-consciousness*, Grtiffin, USA, Reprint 2002.

Rajneesh, Bhagwan (Osho), *Tantra: The Supreme Understanding,* Boulder, Chidvilas, 1993.

Ramanujan, A.K., Velucheru Narayana Rao, David Shulman, *When God Is a Customer—Telugu Courtesan Poems by Ksetrayya and Others*, Oxford University Press, New Delhi, Paperback, *c.*1995.

Reading About the World, Vol. 1, edited by Paul Brians, Mary Gallwey, Douglas Hughes, Azfar Hussain, Richard Law, Michael Myers, Michael Neville, Roger Schlesinger, Alice Spitzer, and Susan Swan, Harcourt Brace Custom Books.

Reddington James (trans./ed.), *The Love Games of Krishna by Vallabhacharya,* Motilal Banarsidass, New Delhi.

Samkara Bhagavatpada, *The Saundarya Lahiri*, The Theosophical Publishing House, Chennai.

Schelling Andrew, *For love of the dark one Mirabai,* Hohm Press, USA,1998.

Scott C. David, *Radha in the Erotic Play of the Universe*, Christian Century magazine March 1, 1995, copyright of The Century Foundation, Bangalore.

Sells Micheal, Professor (trans.), *Tarjuman al-ashwaq (The Interpreter of Desires)* of Mukyiddin Ibn Al-Arabi, Quest Books; Rpt. edition, 1978.

Sharma, Krishna: *Bhakti and the Bhakti Movement*, A New Perspective, Munshiram Manoharlal Publication, New Delhi, 2002.

Shastri, J.L. and G.P. Bhatt (eds.): *Puranic Texts, Ancient Indian Tradition and Mythology,* Vols. 1-4 *Siva Purana*; Vols. 5-6 *Linga Purana* ; Vols. 7-11 *Bhagavata Purana*; Vols. 33–36 *Brahmavaivarta Purana*; Vols. 49-60, Motilal Banarsidass, New Delhi.

Shaw, Miranda, *Passionate Enlightenment (Women in Tantric Buddhism)*, New Delhi, 1998.

Shrila Prabhupada Bhaktivedanta, Book Trust International.

Sircar, D.C., *The Sakti Cult and Tara*, University of Calcutta, Calcutta, 1967.

Spitzer, S.J., Robert, *'Four Levels of Happiness,'* unpublished lecture (1999).

Sri Aurobindo, *The Adventure of Consciousness*, Harper Collins, New Delhi, 1974.

Subramanian, V.K., *Saundaryalahari of Adi Shankracharya*, Motilal Banarsidass, Delhi, 2001.

Tagare, Ganesh Vasudeo, *Bhagavata Purana or Bhagavatam,* Ancient Indian Tradition & Mythology Series, Vol. 10, Motilal Banarsidass, Delhi, 1978.

Tharu, Susie and Lalita, K. (eds.), Women Writing in India Vol. 1,600 BC to the Early Twentieth Century, Oxford University Press, New Delhi, 1991.

Tigunait, Pandit Rajmani, *Sakti, The Power in Tantra*, Himalayan Inst. Press, Pennsylvania, June 1999.

Turner, Katherine S. H., 'From Classical to Imperial: Changing Visions of Turkey in the Eighteenth Century.' In Steve Clark (ed.), *Travel Writing and Empire: Postcolonial Theory in Transit,* London & New York: Zed, 1999.

Varma, Pavan and Sandhya Mulchandani, *Love and Lust: An Anthology of Erotic Ancient and Medieval Indian Literature*, Harper Collins, New Delhi, 2001.

'Vidyakara: Cameos of Wisdom,' Eloise Hart *Sunrise Magazine*, September 1970, Theosophical University Press, US.

Vidyapati Padavali, Translated by Ananda K. Coomaraswamy and Arun Sen, 1994.

Viswanathan Peterson, Indira translation of *Campantar [Sambandar]*, 6th-7th century *Poems to Shiva: The Hymns of the Tamil Saint*, Princeton Library, 1989.

W.T. de Bary (trans) *Cittavisuddhiprakarana* of Aryadeva, *The Buddhist Tradition,* Vintage Books, New York, 1972.

W.T. de Bary, *The Buddhist Tradition,* Vintage Books, New York, 1972.

Wayman, A., *The Yoga of the Guhyasamaja Tantra: The Arcane Lore of Forty Verses*, Motilal Banarsidass, New Delhi, 1977.

Wayman, Alex, *Yoga of the Guhyasamaja Tantra*, Motilal Banarsidass, Delhi, 1977.

Winternitz, M., *Notes on the Guhyasamaja Tantra and the Age of the Tantras*, IHQ, Calcutta, 1933.

Winters, Jonah, 'Themes of The Erotic in Sufi Mysticism,' published essay in Baha'I academics resource library.

Woodroffe, Sir John and Muchyopahdyaya, *Mahamaya, the World as Power, Power as Consciousness,* Ganesh and Co., Madras, 1964.

———, *Hymns to the Goddess,* Ganesh and Co., Madras, 1973.

———, *Introduction to Tantra Shastra*, Ganesh and Co., Madras, 1956.

———, *Kamakalavilasa* (in English translation), Ganesh and Co., Madras, 1953.

Zimmer, Heinrich, *Myths and Symbols in Indian Art and Civilization*, Edited by Joseph Campbell, Bollingen Series/Pantheon/Random House, New York, 1946.

photo credits

CORBIS
2, 127, 166, 183, 190-191

FITZWILLIAM MUSEUM, UNIVERSITY OF CAMBRIDGE, UK
14, 15, 88, 120-121, 172-173, 176

LANCE DANE
1, 26, 27, 50-52, 66-67, 96, 97, 138, 141-143, 146,
148, 149, 151, 162, 165, 171, 184-185

M.D. SHARMA: 19

ORIENTAL MUSEUM, UNIVERSITY OF DURHAM
64, 106a, 106b, 107a, 107b, 128a, 128b, 129a, 129b, 168, 169

PRIVATE COLLECTIONS
101, 144, 147, 155

PRIVATE COLLECTION / BRIDGEMAN ART GALLERY
4, 36-37, 38, 54a, 54b, 55a, 55b, 102, 111, 114, 116-119, 123, 132, 133

ROLI BOOKS PRIVATE COLLECTION
5, 6, 8, 11, 12a, 13b, 20-23, 24a, 24b, 25a, 25b, 28, 30-31, 33,
34, 40, 41, 43, 44, 46, 47, 53, 58, 59, 60, 61, 63, 70, 71, 73, 74, 76,
78-79, 82, 83, 90, 92, 93, 95, 108-109, 112, 113, 124, 125,
130, 131, 134, 135, 137, 152, 153, 157, 161,
174, 175, 178-179, 192

VICTORIA & ALBERT MUSEUM, LONDON
12b, 16, 17, 56, 68, 69, 89, 98, 104-105, 158, 163, 180

✻ *Following pages 190-191:* Whatever path one chooses to
walk, the final goal shall always remain attaining sublime bliss.

ISBN: 978-81-7436-384-8

© This edition Roli & Janssen BV 2007
Second impression
Published in India by Roli Books
in arrangement with Roli & Janssen BV
The Netherlands
M-75 Greater Kailash II (Market)
New Delhi 110 048, India
Ph: ++91-11-29212782, 29210886
Fax: ++91-11-29217185
E-mail: roli@vsnl.com
Website: rolibooks.com

Design: Arati Subramanyam
Layout: Naresh Mondal
Production: Naresh Nigam

Printed and bound in Singapore